Praise for *The Reluctant Messenger*

"A must-read book that highlights the author's spiritual journey into the unknown. It is uplifting, inspiring, and transformative." — **Rajiv Parti, MD, NDE expert, consultant in consciousness-based healing, and author of** *Dying to Wake Up*

"I am fascinated with the detailed messages that Candice has received from her celestial team of advisors. This is a captivating account of expanded awareness that includes gems of spiritual wisdom, messages from her nonphysical mentors, and, in her words, 'uncanny shards of knowledge.'" — **William Buhlman, leading authority on out-of-body experiences, author of** *The Secret of the Soul, How to Have an Out-of-Body Experience, Higher Self Now!,* **and the international best seller** *Adventures Beyond the Body*

"This extraordinary book, filled with wisdom, is the result of a revolution that took place in author Candice Sanderson's life. She was an ordinary person who, by being open and accepting, allowed messages from another realm to come through to her. She courageously faced her own doubt, fear, and judgment as she was shown truths about creation, time, and other profound topics. This is a book for people who seek answers to the nature of our existence. This is a book that needs to be savored, not just read." — **Roberta Moore, producer of spiritual films**

"Candice Sanderson takes us on a journey that in times past was reserved only for initiates laboring in the secret confines of mystery schools. But this book demonstrates that what was once available to only a select few is now happening spontaneously to ordinary (and sometimes reluctant) people. It is a harbinger of things to come. If you want an advance glimpse into the next stage of human evolution, read this book!" — **Paul Rademacher, former executive** director of The Monroe Institute and author of *A Spiritual Hitchhiker's Guide to the Universe*

"Candice Sanderson opens a doorway for all of us to a profound spiritual dimension where verifiable information and answers abound. Follow Candice's steps beyond the threshold of the rational mind to receive powerful messages that eagerly await you!" — **John Kortum, medical intuitive and author of *The Kortum Technique***

"In the spirit of Carl Jung's *Red Book* and Philip K. Dick's *Exegesis,* Candice Sanderson recounts her inner experiences and thoughts in an easygoing narrative that gradually moves readers beyond physical reality. *The Reluctant Messenger* outlines the progression of her spiritual development, from an initial apprehension of the unknown to the cultivation of an openness that leads her to becoming a 'messenger' heralding the raising of human consciousness. Her book also introduces and explains concepts such as the nature of vibration and energy and how time is perceived. Her most touching description, though, is of her being shown how to acknowledge the spiritual life within a plant before cutting one of its flowers. *The Reluctant Messenger* is an interesting read and one with the ability to teach its readers new things about the world in which we live." — **Mark Hunter Brooks, author of *Christianity from a Different Perspective***

"An unlikely messenger stumbles across a vast expanse of enlightenment when a singular message of insight and intrigue drops into her mind, literally out of the blue, on the way to her day job as a psychologist. Her traditional training in conventional psycho-analytics did not prepare her for the turn of events that would suddenly alter her life and understanding of all-that-is, forever. She hadn't asked for it, didn't seek it, and certainly wasn't expecting it, but she was compelled to explore the ever-stranger turn of psychic events that were happening to her, seemingly of their own volition.

"Intrigued by a voice she knew was not hers, delivering a message of wisdom she knew she could not have made up, Candice Sanderson made a decision to pick up the thread and follow it. Little did she know that following that thread would lead her into immense regions of universal consciousness imparting wisdom—wisdom that would not only impact her but also transform those around her—and reveal astounding knowledge.

"With an easy narrative that is right away invitational and informative, Sanderson, with the help of her Guides, parts the veil of existential mysteries and reveals them as practical, down-to-earth truths. Reading *The Reluctant Messenger* sheds light on the mystery and weirdness of why we exist in the first place. This book is instantly approachable and ultimately satisfying as an exposé of what it means to be human on this planet, at this time, in this age."
— **Laurin Bellg, MD, award-winning author of international best seller,** *Near Death in the ICU: Stories from Patients Near Death and Why We Should Listen to Them*

"*The Reluctant Messenger* is a gift from a spiritual dimension. You will not find this unique perspective elsewhere. As I process passages from each chapter, I notice that references are beginning to weave into my life, and I can really feel my creativity igniting, visually like a quiet, steady sparkler from July 4th. Reading this book could be the bridge to your expanded consciousness!" — **Gayle Santone, spiritualist**

"Incredible! Candice Sanderson's book, *The Reluctant Messenger*, is a fascinating exploration into spiritual realms." — **Maria Ashmore, psychologist**

"Be prepared for a complete and radical change in the way you view reality." — **Allyn Evans, author of** *Live a Powerful Life,* **founder of Energy Medicine Squared**

the

RELUCTANT MESSENGER

· Tales from Beyond Belief ·

AN ORDINARY PERSON'S EXTRAORDINARY JOURNEY INTO THE UNKNOWN

Greg,
Listen to the beat of your
heart. Follow.
Love,
Candice M.
Sanderson

Candice M. Sanderson

CLARK PRESS

An Imprint of Crystalline Wisdom Path, LLC
Naples, Florida

Parties interested in quantity sales or autographed copies may contact Clark Press through the author's webpage at www.CandiceSanderson.com.

Published by Clark Press, Naples, Florida
Clark Press is an imprint of Crystalline Wisdom Path, LLC

Cover design by MaryDes www.MaryDes.eu
Editorial assistance by Jennifer Razee
Interior design and formatting by SapphireBookEditing.com
Author photo by Dr. Neil Cohen

The Reluctant Messenger: Tales from Beyond Belief / Candice M. Sanderson. — 1st ed.

Library of Congress Control Number: 2017918547

ISBN 978-0-9996427-0-2 (paperback)
ISBN 978-0-9996427-1-9 (ebook)
ISBN 978-0-9996427-2-6 (hardback)

To Phillip, Cassie, Lorelai, Shalane, Daryl,

and

The Muses Within

"If you want to find the secrets of the universe,

think in terms of energy, frequency, and vibration." — Nikola Tesla

CONTENTS

FOREWORD

When I first met Candice Sanderson nearly a decade ago at a conference that she was co-facilitating, the immediate impression I had of her was, "This is a very practical and pragmatic woman who cares about facts, is extremely organized, and is a straight shooter." My first impressions were correct—this is fundamentally who Candice is, which makes her epic, life-changing journey all the more astonishing.

We became friends at that conference—long before she began to receive unusual messages that she knew were not creations of her own imagination—and remain so to this day. To know Candice personally is to understand that to be a conduit for spiritual messages is just not how she usually operates. By nature, she is a seeker of facts to support provable theory, and as such would naturally be uncomfortable dwelling within a field of experiences she instinctively *knows* to be true, without a reliable way to prove them. This inherent quality of valuing facts above all else makes Candice an ideal, albeit reluctant, messenger.

I recall spending time with her some years ago at a retreat center in Virginia where we were roommates. This was right at the beginning of when she began to receive messages, and I distinctly remember her sharing her early experiences with me with some hesitation. There was a bit of concern on her part that I might not believe her. Far from that—I was witness to her own doubt and amazement at what was happening and the messages she was receiving, which made her experience that much more believable to me.

I've been fortunate enough to hear many of Candice's revelations over the years, long before they were condensed into the book you are now reading. In fact, given the wide swath of varied experiences and unusual phenomena she's encountered, I could not have even begun to imagine how she would collate them into a synthesized anthology with a satisfying story arc that supported a unified shift in fundamental thought. Yet that is exactly what she has done.

I've been honored to be one of the trusted friends invited to read Candice's book throughout its many iterations—both as separate pieces of stand-alone segments jotted down in hurried emails and related in quick phone calls, to the fluid tome that is now released to the world—and each time I do, I receive something different that influences not only my view of *the way things are,* but also how I view myself and my place in this wild and wonderfully mysterious universe. The ability to present a timelessly relevant and lasting message that continues to reveal fresh insights each time it is read is an art, and Candice does it well.

This book is eminently readable. While the concepts and insights revealed herein are potentially heady and abstract, Candice's practical side comes through for us and paves the way to an easier understanding of what has been imparted to her to share with us. In addition to being someone who treasures truth and provable facts, she also has a distinct intolerance for extraneous and unnecessary information. Her modus operandi has always been and remains, "Give it to me straight and spare me the unnecessary details." Because I know this about her, the fact that Candice was able to enter into a space where a comprehension of what she was receiving was often gentle, slow, and frequently not easily understood, reinforces just how remarkable these experiences are.

The pace at which the author lets us observe her unusual journey allows us to stretch our ability to believe her story in a comfortable and accommodating way, without necessarily increasing our capacity to consider it as fundamental truth crumbling in on itself. It is a gently unfolding story of incredible *tales from beyond belief* that invites us to consider in a logical and credible way that we are truly more than strictly physically restricted, earthbound biological matter, and it helps us understand that we are actually more spiritual than physical. We just don't easily remember that part of ourselves—yet.

Candice reveals messages to us just as she received them, totally unedited and copied straight from her journals and transcribed from recordings, and it works: you really do get the sense that you are walking beside her in her own personal journey as it unfolds.

The experiences she shares in *The Reluctant Messenger* seem simple at first, and then they become ever more complex and mind-blowing. From the very first insight that she received—how a flower can bloom so easily, without effort or constraint, because it is, by its very nature, a *flow-er*—to the heady concept that we are actually all one by way of connection through a fluid crystalline grid that is at once everywhere and in everything, we evolve in our understanding of the nature of things right along with the author.

Once, after a meditation during another event Candice and I were attending together, she emerged from deep reflection with a sense of amazement and excitement over a download of information she had received while deeply submerged in an exploration of consciousness and vast inner space. It seemed to be a random collection of isolated facts about a recently deceased man. It was detailed and distinct information: first name, last name, city and state where he had lived, the company name where he had been employed. She had no previous knowledge of any of this information, and she was in no way related to this person, either by blood or circumstance. While I just felt peaceful during the meditation we had just completed and so relaxed I knew I would sleep well that night, Candice had received an incredibly detailed message seemingly out of thin air, with no predisposed motivation or specific inquiry.

With a sense of awe and anticipation, we both huddled around her laptop as we dared to do an Internet search of the information she had received from her meditation. I am at a loss to adequately express the sense of wonder and total befuddlement we both experienced as we found this man's obituary online. As we worked our way through the details of his death announcement, we were speechless as each fact Candice received was confirmed, down to his place of employment—information she had received during meditation. She had no connection to this man whatsoever, and there was no feasible way she could have had access to his personal information beforehand. It was truly mysterious and exciting that Candice had received this information for no obvious reason that we could discern at the time.

To experience this unusual moment with Candice as it actually happened was remarkable, and I was excited to see, as I read her book, that the spirit of that moment was anchored throughout the entire text of *The Reluctant Messenger*. Knowing Candice as I do and experiencing the authenticity of the moment when she realized that the information she had received about a deceased man in Kansas was based in a reality that she did not and could not have known beforehand was powerful. For the reader now embarking on that continued journey with her, the power of that connection with things unseen and the wisdom that emanates from it continue.

Laurin Bellg, MD

Award-winning author of the international best seller, *Near Death in the ICU: Stories from Patients Near Death and Why We Should Listen to Them*

INTRODUCTION

In ten minutes, my life changed forever. My comfortable six decades of living became unrecognizable. Change brings different perspectives, and I soon discovered I questioned everything I knew, or thought I knew, about life.

I had moved from Kentucky to Naples, Florida, in 1993. My husband had died in 1987, and I was left to raise both children without him. My life felt like a whirlwind as I tried to balance my new role as a single parent while working full time to keep food on the table. By the time I left Kentucky six years later, things had settled. Phillip had graduated from college and was working in the music industry in Nashville, Tennessee. Cassie had just finished third grade when we packed our bags and headed south. Soon, we had acclimated to our new lifestyles as Floridians.

I began working in Naples as a psychologist in the public schools. The work is often challenging and demanding. As a member of an emergency team, I travel to schools to provide support for students and staff during crises such as the death of a student or staff member. I also conduct violent threat assessments—something that seems increasingly necessary these days. A large portion of my work includes psychological evaluations and counseling to students in need. I consult with teachers on behavior management techniques and academic intervention support in addition to providing district-wide training for several state and federal programs for students with disabilities. Whether it was helping teachers, students, or peers, my career choice as a psychologist fulfilled my life-long desire to help others.

Fast forward to 2013: My children were grown with kids of their own. My life had settled into a predictable yet rewarding routine; I was perfectly happy. I went to work each day, came home, read a book, and talked on the phone or sat in front of some sort of electronic screen. As I look back on my life then, nothing appeared out of the ordinary—not in the way I dressed and spoke, or in my habits, work, friendships, or thoughts. As a psychologist, I differentiated normal from abnormal, and my life represented nothing but the commonplace. My training as a psychologist had prepared me, or so I thought, for the challenges that life presented. That was about to change.

Planning for an average but busy day occupied my mind as I gathered my belongings and headed toward the car one morning. The summer break had ended just a few weeks before, and school was back in full swing. As I exited the garage, I began to mentally prioritize tasks leading up to the back-to-back meetings for the day. Almost on autopilot, I began my fifteen-minute commute. It was dark; the sun would not rise for another forty-five minutes or so. The traffic was usually light this early in the morning, and today was no exception. I had driven about halfway when words that did not seem to come from any conscious thought began to flow through my mind. My purse was in the passenger's seat. I reached over and brought it closer so I could feel inside for my phone. I wanted to record these thoughts. When I could not safely reach the phone, I gave up and yielded to the message.

August 28, 2013

When you look at a flower, it is at its peak when it is open. A flower is a flow-er, and just like a human, when you let the energy flow, then the human is open to growth and potential. A plant draws energy from deep within Mother Earth, and it then ascends toward Father Sky. When there is perfect connection, this union between Mother Earth and Father Sky, the plant's energy is in ideal alignment. Its energy is flowing, and there are no blockages. It will then burst forth from its current existence and produce a perfect blossom, a flower.

The plant is a flow-er of energy, and its perfect alignment with Source results in a flower. This is also true for humans. When humans allow their energy to flow, they open to potential growth beyond their wildest imaginations. The result is a perfect flower—beautiful, functional, and multifaceted. Let us all be flow-ers of energy, with no blockages.

As these words entered my awareness, a picture of a green plant formed in my mind. Its roots extended deep in rich, dark soil as it began to grow upward. Like a time-lapsed movie, I saw a bud form and then open into a beautiful yellow flower.

I felt shocked. What was this? My breath quickened, and my heart pounded. This was so strange. As a psychologist, I questioned whether this could be an auditory hallucination—that I was perceiving voices that were not there. I quickly ran through the basic criteria for hallucinations, and I had none of them: mental illness (bipolar, schizophrenia, psychosis), dementia, psychedelic drug use, or seizure disorders.

The message ended and left me with silence and thoughts that I knew were once again my own. I began to analyze this experience. Father Sky? Mother Earth? These words were not mine, nor were the thoughts, so I could dismiss this as something that came *from* me. I had ruled out hallucinations, but what was it? Was this one of those mystical experiences that I had read about? I had no idea.

As I looked back at my initial physical reactions—my heart pounding and my breath quickening—I must have felt fear, but my analysis of the message revealed there was nothing negative about it. In fact, it seemed to have only positive attributes. I smiled broadly as I realized this was *awesome*. It was as though I had peeked into some unknown, magical space. The mystery of the words played over and over in my mind as I continued my commute to work, surrounded by a sense of wonder of what had just occurred.

I arrived at my assigned school and drove into the staff parking area. The elementary school's lighted parking lot was empty, with the exception of the office manager's car. I gathered my briefcase and my personal belongings and headed toward the building's side entrance that led directly to the guidance suite, where my office was located. With building keys in hand, as I walked from the parking lot, a royal poinciana—a tree I had probably passed a hundred times before—demanded my attention. Its graceful, widely spreading branches that curved from a gnarly trunk seemed to beckon me. As the morning sun peeked through the tree's fern-leafed canopy, the rays produced mesmerizing patterns of shadow and light on the ground. As I gazed at the tree, I realized it was not just a living tree, but a sentient being—as much alive as I was. I stood still and was admiring the tree's beauty when my focus shifted to a tiny bud amid the tree's orange-red blossoms. My thoughts returned to the words: *"Let us all be flow-ers of energy."* I knew I had been guided to the tree to see this unopened bud.

Although I could not explain how the message and the experience with the tree had occurred, I knew something significant had just happened. I felt I had accessed a mysterious and perhaps mystical realm. I took a deep breath and sent my gratitude to the tree. I walked away not with answers but questions: Did this bud represent me—an untapped potential waiting to blossom? If I heeded the advice to be grounded and in alignment, would my life flow as well? Would I burst into bloom like the tree? Was this a once-in-a-lifetime event, or would it happen again?

This first message had turned my world upside down. It represented a beginning, the cracking of a door into a world of the unknown. Yet as strange as the events had felt, I settled back into my normal routine. I went to work as usual, and I was soon involved in the daily activities that had consumed my life before the experience. I spent my weekends recovering from the workweek and talking on the phone or visiting with Phillip and Cassie. Although always in the back of my mind, the experience began to fade within the daily routines of my life.

On September 12, I received a message from a friend who had passed away, followed by a steady stream of similar communications. What had been neatly tucked away as a once-in-a-lifetime experience came center stage. The significance of these messages began to weigh on my mind because they were different—they were meant for others. This was a pivotal moment for me as I recognized I was being asked to *share* the messages. *Becoming* the messenger presented much greater challenges than simply receiving them.

As I tried to sort out these new events, I felt more than a little overwhelmed. My initial shock at becoming a messenger rendered me without a plan, so I listened and recorded. By default, I remained opened, and this laid the groundwork for more messages to flow. After much thought and deliberation, I began to realize the impact the onslaught of these new communications had on me. The messages had thrust me into this new role of messenger—without my consent—yet deep within the recesses of my mind whispered a voice of reason, and I knew this was the right thing to do.

At one time, I belonged to an online meditation group that encouraged many interesting philosophical discourses on expanded awareness and other similar topics. One evening the task was to gather information about human consciousness. Does human consciousness have the ability to learn, and if so, how can we develop it? While responding to this nebulous prompt, I felt the familiar shift in awareness as a message came through, and I watched as content spilled onto my computer screen from my keyboard. I never gave this experience much thought until a couple years later, when I attended a workshop at The Monroe Institute in Faber, Virginia.

As the first session of the training ended, a man approached me and introduced himself as Fred. He had a soft smile and a twinkle in his eyes as he reached into his hip pocket for his wallet. He opened the wallet and pulled out a tattered piece of paper. Without explanation, yet maintaining eye contact, he offered it to me. I read it, looked into this stranger's eyes, and smiled—it was my online entry.

The message detailed humanity's progression toward harmony. The last paragraph read, "The evolution of your species will be in the direction of more highly sensitive beings. It is happening even now, whether you encourage it or not. All over the world, people are beginning to wake up and re-member who they truly are. To help this process, learn to trust what your body tells you, not your mind. Allow the truth to unfold. Do not *try* to do anything, but learn to let it flow and accept what you receive."

I began to recognize the impact some of the messages had on others: I did not even remember this post, yet a complete stranger had printed it and carried it in his wallet. I didn't know the meaning that it held for Fred, only that it was important to him. But I understood how he felt, because I had experienced the gentle tug of these communications that called me to explore worlds I never knew existed, to see connections, and to understand there is more to life than what I had thought.

Was this another reminder for me to step into the role as messenger? I didn't feel like a *reluctant* messenger—more like a *terrified* one—yet I felt a nagging sensation that dragged me, sometimes kicking and screaming, to accept this unsought position. So, I began to tell my story to others.

At first, I told a few friends about the messages; they were supportive and often eager to hear more. This sharing seemed to open the door for more people to explore. Shortly after I met Fred, the leader of The Monroe Institute's Local Chapter Network asked me to become a regular contributor to their online quarterly newsletter. As I began to share my experiences through this international venue, I realized that what had begun as private communications meant for me alone or just a few friends had expanded beyond my expectations. My circle had grown as I collaborated with larger audiences, and I traveled beyond the self-imposed limits that had constrained me in the past.

As the audience widened, however, so did the reactions. Although I had worked through much of my initial fear and doubt about exposing these very personal experiences, sometimes my discomfort with being a messenger resurfaced.

In fact, not long ago, I accompanied my daughter, Cassie, and her husband, Dan, to a cookout at Dan's parent's house. Several families were there, and children were running around, happy to be playing with their cousins. The toddlers occupied themselves at a water table area while the older children jumped in and out of the swimming pool. People meandered between the covered lanai and the granite island bar—which held generous offerings of delicious appetizers—just inside the opened sliding glass doors to the kitchen. Both inside and out, I heard laughter and lively conversations as people greeted each other and shared the latest family news.

Dan's sister and her husband welcomed me with a hug. Through Cassie and Dan, they knew I had been writing a book, so as polite conversation goes, they asked me about the book's topic. As I responded to this simple question, I realized they were unaware of the book's subject—and apparently uncomfortable with its esoteric nature. Dan's sister's mouth dropped open, and her eyes widened as I fumbled to describe my experiences. I recognized her fear, so I tried to give details that, in my opinion, might convince her that these messages were genuine. But it seemed the more I tried to explain, the more frightened she became. Her reaction brought a flood of tears to my eyes—so in the middle of this celebratory gathering of family and friends, I cried.

Why couldn't I have just acknowledged her fear? Why couldn't I have told her that I understood her feelings, because initially I had felt the same way? I recalled how my heart had pounded and I had felt breathless, but why couldn't I have told her that soon, very soon, comfort, curiosity, and even awe replaced my shock and disbelief? After all, I had learned valuable lessons from the messengers, and my life had changed for the better.

The more important question, however, was why was I upset over her reaction? I should have never tried to share what she was not ready to hear. I certainly should have never tried to convince her of anything, because truths discovered are uniquely our own, and each person's truth should be honored.

Now when doubt or fear of being a messenger creeps into my awareness, I think of Fred's printed copy of my online post. If the messages were important to him, perhaps they would be for others, too. So I gradually acquiesced to my role as messenger.

As I look back on this journey that had begun with a message about a flower, I realize how far I have traveled this path of the unknown. Message by message, day by day, how I viewed the world changed. Something nebulous guided me, and I could no longer define the events in my life by what my physical senses measured. I realized this synergistic process had unanticipated results: I had accepted the role of messenger—I had become a *"flower of energy."*

CHAPTER 1: THE MUSES WITHIN

It was the middle of the night, and I had been driving for hours. When I made a fuel stop, I got lost. The interstate's closed on-ramp detoured traffic on meandering back roads to reach the next exchange. I could see the interstate, but I couldn't get there. After multiple attempts to reach the on-ramp, I stopped my car and again tried to decipher the GPS on my phone. It kept rerouting me to the closed on-ramp. I cried.

Headlights appeared in my rearview mirror. My heart pounded with anxiety, then I felt relief as a woman my age, dressed in medical scrubs, came to my aid. I scribbled her directions on the back of an envelope I had found deep inside my purse. Step-by-step instructions—it seemed easy enough to follow.

I took a deep breath, dried my eyes, and adjusted my seatbelt. Before leaving, I turned to thank the woman who rescued me, but she had disappeared. Gone. Not a trace of her or her car. I knew I had not imagined her, because I held the proof in my hands—the directions to safety.

I woke to realize I'd been dreaming. I should have recognized the precognitive qualities of this dream—when I least expected it, help would come—but I did not.

I had learned a valuable lesson after the incident with the flower and the royal poinciana tree: setting aside judgment and doubt resulted in an open invitation for more messages. Soon, I was inundated with messages.

They came in different formats; the most common was dictation. Not only did I hear the words, but what punctuation to use, where to place quotation marks, start a new paragraph, capitalize letters, or insert parentheses. Sometimes I heard, "Strike that," if I made a mistake, followed by the corrected word or phrase. (Because of this precision, I edited very little; most of the messages in the book are verbatim, even if I did not agree with the word usage or punctuation.)

Other times I received collections of information that came all at once, whole and complete, like a computer download. If possible, I tried to capture these messages while at my computer to eliminate the extra step of transcribing from my phone's recorder.

At times, either still or moving images accompanied the more difficult-to-understand messages to ensure my comprehension. As these played in my mind's eye, they added clarity beyond the spoken word. I watched as symbols, numbers, or words appeared one character at a time on a whiteboard. Sometimes I saw events with multiple people, just like a movie. At times, I observed. Other times, I participated in the events and, oddly enough, sometimes I did both.

When I saw myself in these visions, all my senses operated fully. I felt the wind on my face and the grass beneath my feet. I watched white clouds drift against a blue sky as insects buzzed past me and birds sang in the distance. Stray whiffs from blooming flowers permeated the air, and I smelled the earthy, refreshing scent of nearby pine trees. When detailed images accompanied a message, they always repeated, even if I reviewed the transcripts months later. Although these "internal videos" did not change, I had control over some of the functions; I could pause, rewind, and even fast-forward.

Some messages came to me through just "knowing." They were similar to downloads in their content, but the elusive, subtle, and indirect method of delivery allowed me to sense the communication. Often, it was specific, such as a name or geographic location. I cannot explain how—I just *knew* the information.

Sometimes I had a preview of coming attractions, a sort of cosmic heads-up. Errant thoughts would drop into my awareness at the oddest times—as I showered, when I dressed for work, or even in my dreams. I came to understand that these were introductions to topics that would arrive when I set aside sufficient time to receive them.

These messages began to arrive daily, and they flowed as easily as the first one had. Many of the early communications occurred during my commute to work. It seems that having my recorder on offered some sort of silent invitation because as soon as I got into my car, fastened my seatbelt, and turned on the recorder, things started to happen. And because I was concentrating on something else, like my driving, my conscious mind didn't block what was ready to come forth. Before long, this pattern proved successful, and my journal began to fill with communications from multiple messengers.

A couple of weeks after the initial message, I began to receive communications from people who had passed away. These messages would often make no sense to me but would have significance for their family or friends. I had known about mediums and their uncanny ability to connect with people who had passed, but I had never expected to be one.

On September 12, 2013, the first of these messages came from my friend Becky, a kindergarten teacher who had died several years before. She had a message for Marie, a mutual friend and coworker. Becky said Marie would have a health issue in the near future, but she should stay strong, and all would be well. Becky wanted Marie to know she watches over her, and she should not be afraid.

Four days later I received information from a coworker's son who had passed sixteen months before. At the age of thirty-six, this young man whom I will call John died from a degenerative disease that left him physically disabled. He told me he had chosen this life, and all his experiences were rich, especially having two loving parents who "gave and gave and gave" to make his life comfortable. He acknowledged his mother's regrets that he did not have the typical life experiences such as getting married and having children. John wanted his parents to know how important they were to him—more important than anything else life could have offered. He was healed, strong, and "living in perfection." He kept saying, "All is good. All is good. All is good."

What happened next surprised me. I saw a slab of granite in my mind's eye. I watched as John picked up a tool and chiseled the words, "It's all good." I had misunderstood. And although the difference between "It's all good" and "All is good" may seem inconsequential, details such as these often confirm the authenticity of the messages. I shared this information with a close friend of John's family. She confirmed John's frequent use of this saying. Even when in debilitating pain as his health declined, he always stated, "It's all good."

Less than a week later, on September 19, a friend's daughter contacted me. Although Lyne and I lived in different states, we kept in touch through frequent phone calls. Twelve years ago, there had been a break in our communication, and I wondered why. When we made contact, Lyne told me how her beautiful daughter, Robin, had been murdered by her ex-boyfriend. My heart broke for Robin and especially for the two young children she had left behind.

Robin said she watched over her children, and she was adamant that she had never left them. She told me she held no ill will regarding the circumstances of her passing. She acknowledged that her willingness to release this negativity would be difficult for many to comprehend. I knew that to be true. I had witnessed the aftermath of gut-wrenching grief and anger that her violent passing had created; it would be difficult for those left behind to forgive so readily.

Near the end of the communication, I heard Robin say "Mary Loody." That was an odd name, and I wondered whether I had heard her correctly.

I called Lyne, and we both sobbed as I shared Robin's message. In response to my question about "Mary Loody," Lyne told me about her childhood friend named Mary Lou who went by the nickname Loody. This detail offered proof for Lyne that the message had come from Robin.

I received messages for several friends during the next couple of weeks. The one on September 23 surprised me. It came from Marilyn's father, who had passed away. Marilyn was one of the first people I had met when we moved from Kentucky to Florida in 1993. She was a principal in the same school district where I was later employed. My daughter, Cassie, and Marilyn's daughter, Stephanie, had met in gymnastics class during the first month of our relocation. Though we were newcomers, Marilyn and Stephanie made us feel at home.

The surprise from hearing from Marilyn's father was because he was accompanied by *both* his first wife of almost fifty years and his second wife of seventeen years. Doreen had died of a heart attack in 1993, and a couple of years later, Bill married Wilma Lee. Both Bill and Wilma Lee were 89 when they passed in 2010: Bill passed in May, followed by Wilma Lee in September.

Because all three had attended the same high school in Indiana, Pennsylvania, they knew of one another, but they had not been part of the same circle of friends. Now together in the spirit world, the three were lively, full of energy and laughter as they acknowledged they were together on the "other" side.

I felt somewhat uncomfortable with a family reunion with multiple spouses. They offered an explanation, perhaps in reaction to my uneasiness. They told me they had "traveled together for many lifetimes" as souls on the same path.

Marilyn's mother, Doreen, interjected that Bill needed two women to keep him under control and added, "He's always been that way." All three laughed at her remarks, suggesting our sense of humor remains intact when we pass away. I had never met Doreen, but I got the impression she had a gentle, quiet energy in direct contrast to her sometimes-surprising sense of humor. All three were happy and content, enjoying being together.

They wanted me to convey to Marilyn that they were with her and her daughter, Stephanie. They told me they were giving Stephanie an "extra layer of love and protection." They said they were doing well and that Wilma Lee had regained all her faculties. Because Doreen had passed seventeen years before the other two, she had helped both Bill and Wilma Lee acclimate to the other side. Then Marilyn's mother stepped forward with a specific message. She wanted to confirm something that had occurred after her passing: Marilyn had seen her.

I called Marilyn and shared the information from her father, mother, and stepmother. We discussed our curiosity about afterlife reunions with multiple spouses. I then broached the subject about Marilyn seeing her mother *after* she had passed. Although the incident had occurred more than twenty-five years ago, it still had a significant impact on Marilyn, who told me the following story.

After checking her baggage at Southwest Florida International Airport in Fort Myers, Florida, Marilyn looked up and saw her mother walking toward an escalator. Marilyn recognized her mother's blond hair, her familiar outfit of shorts and a top, and even her fast-paced walk. Marilyn rushed to catch up as Doreen approached the up escalator to access the airport's gates.

Marilyn described how her heart had pounded as she tried to catch her mother. When she reached the top of the escalator and looked around, her mother was nowhere to be found. Had she vanished, or had she simply disappeared into the crowd?

Marilyn felt conflicted. She knew her mother had died, so her brain told her that it could not have been her, but her heart insisted otherwise. Tears formed in her eyes at the thought that she had lost the opportunity to see her mother one last time.

Doreen's confirmation brought Marilyn again to tears. Her mother's passing had created many sleepless nights and a great sadness for Marilyn. She had needed validation that, on some level, her mother continued to be with her. Doreen said she had been given an opportunity to show herself to Marilyn to confirm their continued mother-daughter connection.

From what I understood from Doreen, such manifestations are uncommon; visitations are more likely to occur during dreams. On rare occasions, however, some souls are granted permission to project their energy in a manner that would allow others to see them. There is some sort of approval process, but, unfortunately, I couldn't understand any further details.

The next day I received a group message for another friend, Ellen. Gathered together were Ellen's mother and two others named Eleanor and Ruth. The communication from these sweet spirits indicated they wanted Ellen to know they were with her and sending her their love. When I called Ellen that night, she identified Ruth and Eleanor as her aunts. She told me that this day had been very difficult for her, and knowing her mom and her two aunts were with her offered her some solace in the midst of the day's challenges.

These new messages defied logical explanation, but soon the winds shifted, and I found myself needing to adjust the sails as a different set of communications arrived. With each new message, I felt like Hansel and Gretel, following a path of cosmic breadcrumbs that led me farther away from ordinary life as I traveled beyond limits that had held me in the past.

Throughout these unfolding communications, I continued to document my interactions, and my journal soon exceeded 150 pages of single-spaced text. Each passing week brought more twists and turns to my extraordinary adventure.

Although I knew others were reading my work in the online newsletter and that my journal had grown exponentially, the idea of writing a book never occurred to me. I had not even considered it until one day in August 2015, two years after the initial message about the flower.

I strolled the coastline of the Gulf of Mexico one morning as the gentle surf lapped at my bare feet. It was quiet and much too early for the beach crowd. Birds called in the distance as I ambled this paradise that I felt lucky to call my home. I began to contemplate the most recent messages.

Information came from multiple messengers, and I often recognized repeat performers by their familiar word usage, topics covered, or their rhythmic language patterns. But these past few days' conversations had differed; I felt as if a friend had stopped by to chat. It was direct, personal dialogue, and it had nothing to do with the greater good for humanity. A different messenger had arrived. Once I returned home, my unasked questions were answered.

August 1, 2015

As this one [me] walked the beach this morning, she was curious about the recent messages she has been receiving. Her thoughts were that this was a new set of energy that she has tapped into. Yes, we tell her. She can refer to us as The Muses Within, for we represent those energies of song, dance, and poetry. We will be helping her as she writes her book. In fact, it is our energy that has been behind the thoughts that have been given to her about writing.

We tell her all she needs to do is to let go of any blocks that she might have, and let us take over. We know the flow; we are the flow. We bypass any blockages with our lighthearted energy. We love that word "lighthearted," for it is of Light as well as of the Heart's energy, which is love.

The book is already written in our realm, and the stories for the book have been well documented by this one in her realm. All that is needed is an intertwining of the dimensions, and the book will be presented to her.

Write, Dear One, in small stages and from your heart. If you become stuck, get up and take leave. The answers will come to you if you take the energy of your attention away from the book. When your energy is so intense and intent upon its subject, then you are not opened to hear our suggestions and direction of flow. For it is truly all about the flow. It is the flow of words upon pages. It is the flow of the story. It is the flow of energy. It is the flow of the flower, the flow-er of information which we gave to you so long ago. Allow us in your field of awareness to guide you.

This is all for now. Know that we are like soft music playing in the background of your life. Take a deep breath, release all tension, and then you are in the perfect space to hear the beautiful music.

The message captivated me; the authors of my first message about a flower had revealed themselves through this familiar lyrical language. And now I had a name for them: The Muses Within. I am not sure why, but having their name brought me a sense of gratification.

But most of the message was about writing a book. Me? Write a book? I had transitioned from receiving messages to sharing messages, but writing a book was a giant step in the sharing process. Was I ready for this? Over the next few days as I processed these questions, I remembered the dream with the step-by-step directions when I was lost. Help had arrived just in time. Was the dream, too, part of this formula—offering help before I even knew I needed it?

Another question entered my mind: Had The Muses Within been responsible for the dream? Was this another example of the gentle guidance from the messengers as they scattered words of truth that whispered to me from below the surface of awareness? So, after much deliberation, I accepted the challenge. Somehow, the task did not seem so daunting with The Muses Within as my copilots—a divine collaborative effort.

It was the first week of August 2015, and my summer break was coming to an end in a few days. It was time to get serious. I sat at my desk, started my computer, and prepared to write the book with The Muses Within as coauthors.

Where to begin? I asked the muses for a title. I waited; nothing happened. I waited longer. Again, nothing happened. What did I expect? Did I think the words would appear on my computer screen? I had not typed a single word, and I felt exhausted. It would have been humorous if it hadn't been so frustrating.

The realization of my first round of writer's block opened a door of awareness, and the muses' words returned to me: *"The answers will come to you if you take the energy of your attention away from the book."* Willing to try anything, I took a deep breath and stood up to take a break from a task that had not yet begun.

Within a few minutes, I felt the pressure of a flood of words swirling around the fringes of my awareness. Like a participant on a television game show with a giant wheel of possibilities spinning in front of me, the wheel stopped. I had asked for a title, and my answer arrived: *The Reluctant Messenger: Tales from Beyond Belief.* The title fit, especially the reluctant part.

So, this is how it will work, I thought. The book would be a collaborative effort between The Muses Within and me. It would not be write-on-demand, but instead a process that the muses intended for us to follow together. I thought, Let the games begin!

As I began to write the book, I could sense the presence of The Muses Within. Words would enter my awareness, and I would feel a sense of urgency to record them. I searched for a balance between receiving and recording the messages. If I did not start right away, I feared the words would fade, so I had to step out of the way to become the scribe. It was a process that I learned by trial and error, but with each step, it became easier.

A few days later I took a morning walk on the beach. I love this time of day; it is early enough to avoid the searing August South Florida sun. Yesterday's hot sand had cooled overnight and refreshed my bare feet. The gentle surf seemed to awaken from a peaceful night's slumber. I heard a spray of water and looked to see a pod of dolphins playing in the warm waters of the Gulf of Mexico. While immersed in my nature walk, The Muses Within spoke.

August 3, 2015

This one has entered into a space of sacredness. Her path began by allowing well-established belief systems to drop away. It resulted in an expansion of realness beyond her wildest imagination.

I agreed with the message. My beliefs had expanded beyond their previous limits and new vistas opened for me. As more messages arrived, I acknowledged the wisdom they held, and I found my belief systems could no longer support the truths I had known. I couldn't view my reality as narrowly as I had in the past. As I released my outdated opinions, I discovered richer and more fulfilling inner landscapes than I had ever dreamed possible.

I felt like a lone explorer who had discovered a secret passage to the unknown that offered spectacular new vistas. These fresh landscapes not only changed my perspectives on the world but also altered my entire life. Once I entered this magical realm, the world I left behind seemed incomplete in comparison, yet I felt conflicted. Writing a book would make my discovery very public, but I knew within my heart that this was my calling.

As I walked away from the secret entrance to this mysterious world, I knew many unopened doors awaited other explorers. How I defined my life changed with each message, and I learned life could not be measured by what meets the eye. My new perspectives resulted in different understandings of the universe. Although I might never know why or how I had become a messenger, an explorer of consciousness, I wondered if this newly found world offered growth opportunities for others as it had for me.

The next day The Muses Within sent messages accompanied by a vision that looked like scenes from an old Western movie.

August 4, 2015

We have instructed this one to get up and leave the task of writing the book if she becomes blocked. There is a blockage because she is trying too hard. It should not be a matter of trying, but instead a matter of allowing. There is a different energy pattern between trying and allowing. The flow is in opposite directions. When you try to reach inspiration, the energy stems from the denser energies of the Earth plane. You are trying to force those energies upward, for lack of a better term, to connect to inspiration. That takes tremendous energy, and it is neither effective nor efficient.

The energy of allowing is in direct opposition to trying. The energy of allowing begins within. Your individual spark of divinity allows the inspiration (in-spiration) to come to you. It is an open invitation, creating a beacon effect for us to send our energies to this one. Many human philosophers have said, "As above, so below." It is not "As below, so above."

This is something known by artists on the Earth plane. Symphonies, tomes of prose, and masterpieces of visual art have been received by the artists opening and allowing these energies of inspiration to work their magic through their Earthly hands. Yes, we say it is the energy of allowing, not the energy of trying, that gives results.

Two short visions accompanied the message and added clarity. A man staggered against the howling desert wind; he had one arm over his face to protect his eyes from the blinding sand. He searched for water to soothe his parched throat. As an open spigot of water mysteriously appeared, he fell to his knees and grabbed at the water, desperate to drink. The water seemed to go everywhere except his mouth. He tried too hard. The next scene began identically, but this time the man approached the open spigot with cupped hands. The water filled his hands and spilled over onto the ground, providing enough water to quench his thirst.

The lessons seemed obvious: trying too hard was counterproductive. I remembered The Muses Within's initial message about the flow-er of energy. The book would blossom into existence if I allowed the words to flow. With a smile of acknowledgment, I allowed the rest of the message to drift into my awareness:

For many years, mystics on the Earth plane have referred to our dimension as "above" and the Earth plane as "below." Terms are used suggesting directionality, yet the direction of above is actually from within. Within all humans are divine sparks from whence they came. It is their essence, their true spirit, a piece of their true Source. Humans have multiple words to describe their true essence—higher self, divine spark, soul, etc.

The words are not important. The point is that the true self is timeless and formless. It is not the physical body; it is the divine spark that temporarily inhabits the physical body. It is part of all that there is. When humans say, "as above, so below," the "above" refers to the higher, subtler vibrational energies of our dimension. "Below" refers to the denser energy field of the Earth plane. By going within, humans tap into the immense energy field of totality of all there is.

"As above, so below" refers to the commonalities between our higher-dimensional realms and the denser energy realms of the Earth plane. The Earth plane is a mirror of our dimension, but not in fullness. It is only a thought or a shadow of a thought of our dimension. Humans often feel "inspired" when producing art, whether it is music, prose, or something upon a canvas. "Inspired" indicates they are tapping into our field of "in-spirit." They have connected and reached into our dimension where the objects of their artistic endeavors already exist.

Pushing my logical resistance aside, I allowed these words of inspiration to flow through me. I felt myself slipping farther down the rabbit hole. Although I needed a lot of time to comprehend the material, I felt honored to have received it.

Although I continued to channel messages daily, I did not set aside a regular time to write the book, so I put the task on hold. But I knew when ready, I needed only to ask for help from The Muses Within. Their words were always right at the surface, waiting for me to allow them entrance.

Working in the public schools, my summers offered a break as well as an ideal time to start back on the task of completing the book. So, in June 2016, with yet another school year of devoting my energies to students finished, I sat poised in front of my computer, ready for action. I felt like a television director: Ready? Set? Action! I was ready to "go live" as soon as The Muses Within arrived.

Things happened instantly. In my mind's eye, a mist of energy swirled around the room. I knew it represented the energy of The Muses Within. Free-formed clouds wove back and forth as their vibrations matched mine, allowing for open and clear communication. I typed the following:

June 11, 2016

This one is correct. We have been waiting in the background for her to call on us. We are now here, in full force. Ritual and ceremony have played important roles in human history. We ask for ritual when calling us. Set aside time each day to work with us, and you will find efficiency in the words that flow. Setting aside a specific time sets the intent and allows us to enter your center of consciousness, thus helping the communication.

It is all a matter of flow, energy flow.

I found myself taking several deep breaths as I settled into the chair, prepared for the messages to continue. As I typed "It is all a matter of flow, energy flow," the following words came:

We have already started our work. Before deciding to "go live," we were working. We listed the chapters for you, did we not?

When you come to us at the assigned time each day, call upon us, and we will bring forth the words you need to hear. We will guide you on what chapters to work on and how to further organize the work.

The Muses Within had already assisted with the organization and the title for the book, and they had laid the foundation on how this collaboration would work. These new instructions to call upon them at a specific time offered an element of structure to the process of connecting with them.

I woke up earlier than usual the next morning, eager to return to the task that had begun in August 2015: I was ready to finish the book. But before starting, I felt the need to take a walk. Had procrastination set in? As I left home, I felt an inexplicable urge to pick flowers, and I recognized this as a gentle nudge from The Muses Within.

I gathered a variety of blossoms, including bright red hibiscus, deep purple Mexican petunias, a large cluster of waxy, variegated, green- and salmon-colored flowers from a crown of thorns, and a few fragrant white gardenias. I brought the bouquet home and floated them in a crystal bowl of water near my workstation. The reds, purples, and whites seemed to bring the display to life. The paper-thin blossoms of the Mexican petunias contrasted with the thick waxy petals from the crown of thorns. The sweet scent from the gardenia permeated the air.

I looked at the arrangement; it seemed incomplete. I lit a candle and set it beside the fragrant bowl of flowers: earth, water, air, and fire. I recognized my actions as part of the previous day's message about ritual and ceremony. Guidance from The Muses Within set the stage for the main event. I waited in anticipation for The Muses Within to work their magic through me. The reluctant messenger was reluctant no more.

CHAPTER 2: GOOD VIBRATIONS

What if I told you our brains are not what we assume they are? Our brains perform many tasks, but thinking is not one of them. In fact, they do not think at all. That is a fallacy. I learned this information in October 2013.

Six weeks after I had received the initial communication about the flower, I received a set of communiqués that felt like classroom lectures. These messages came in response to a conversation with a friend. The night before, Barbara had shared an interesting story, and the telling of her experience seemed to send a beacon into the universe that requested answers to questions not yet asked.

Barbara, her husband Bob, and I belonged to a monthly meditation group. Prior to the meeting, she told us about her recent genealogy project that covered a couple hundred years of her family lineage. While in the middle of the research, Barbara reported a name "popped" into her head out of nowhere. She fascinated us with her story of how this name held eerie and curious significance for the rest of her research. The next day I received information, not so much about Barbara's remarkable connection, but how it had occurred:

October 10, 2013
Your brain is a receiver with varying levels or degrees of strength, just as a signal from a radio station does not reach each receiver with the

same level of success. To simplify this concept, let us look at the different levels of strength within the human brain:

Level #1, when you think of something: *The incoming energy is subtle, and most humans believe it originated from them. Nothing can originate within, because your brain only receives information like a radio receiver. The subtle energy that reaches the brain goes unnoticed, and the assumption arises that the human thought the idea into existence.*

Let us look at the second degree of strength:

Level #2, when something comes to you: *The energy signal behind this thought is stronger than Level #1. The human acknowledges it did not originate from him or her, but instead, it drifted into their awareness. "Where did that come from?" The increased strength of the signal allowed them to perceive that the thought originated outside of themselves.*

Moving to Level #3, the signal is bold and forceful:

Level #3, when something forces itself into your consciousness: *This signal is strong; the energies are working hard to get the human's attention. The human can recognize the force behind the thought as it snaps into the field of awareness. This energy expands and pushes into the human's awareness.*

As flow-ers of energy, allow your antennae to expand to experience all of these energies. Learn to fine-tune by recognizing these three stages of reception. This is just the beginning. There are other levels of reception.

These straightforward ideas made sense to me. We do have thoughts, but they are not generated by the brain; the brain only receives them. I recalled many times that thoughts had drifted into my awareness, and I had been cognizant that they had not originated from me. What surprised and interested me about this message, however, was the suggestion that we could fine-tune our reception.

First it was the flower message, then hearing from departed souls, and now a lecture about the brain. Why were these communications so different? Had I tuned to different stations?

With my curiosity piqued, I wanted to learn more, and that surprised me. I realized that curiosity had replaced my initial sense of shock from six weeks ago, when the first message had arrived.

October 23, 2013

This one is curious about the differences in messages. It is all a matter of tuning the radio to find the right frequency. In terms of channeling energy systems such as this [receiving messages], this is of a much finer vibration and requires finesse. In Earth terms, humans might perceive this energy as farther away, although that is not accurate. There is recognition of us but only through repeated exposure to our frequency fields. At that point in time, you become familiar with our energy patterns. It is all a matter of your Energy Recognition System that makes this seem familiar. The energy frequency of channeling such as this one is different than that of mediumship, but both frequencies are very subtle.

Many people on the Earth plane receive messages from loved ones who have passed away but discount the message as "wishful thinking." These are the subtle frequencies from Level #1, and the humans think they invented the communication, that they originated the thought. If humans would, as you say, put a "space between their thoughts," they would be more likely to acknowledge true messages when they are received.

Sometimes I found pearls of wisdom hidden in the messages. I recalled the times that I had disregarded messages from loved ones who had passed—I thought that I had invented the communication. Years later, and only after I had become the reluctant messenger, did I begin to entertain the possibility that the previous exchanges were genuine. Learning to trust what our hearts know to be true would strengthen the healing process, especially when we lose someone we love.

It is all a matter of fine-tuning and learning to open awareness in order to receive incoming frequencies. The lighter and less-encumbered the energy body is, the more accurately the messages will be perceived.

Humans have what we call Emotional Guidance Systems. Humans can learn to use this innate tool to help increase their vibratory nature in order to become a better receiver. As the Emotional Guidance System ramps up humans' energy fields, their physical bodies become lighter and less encumbered. These are ideal conditions for allowing humans to perceive other energy systems. And, as these energies are perceived, channels or pathways are initiated, thus making future contact easier because the connections strengthen with subsequent contacts.

This message seemed nebulous to me. As if in response to my thoughts, they offered a more relevant analogy:

This is not unlike the neural pathways in your brain. Your scientists know new pathways are established by engaging in new behaviors. Humans who have had strokes are able to regain skills by establishing new pathways that bypass injured areas in the brain. Connection to energy beyond the physical body is a similar process.

This example was easier for me to understand. In graduate school I had studied neuroplasticity, when an injured brain bypasses damaged areas to build new neural circuits. Building neural pathways is the foundation for all learning.

A brief Internet search revealed several sites that helped explain the concept of neuroplasticity by comparing the human brain to radio tuners. Studies performed by Dr. Ehud Ahissar, professor of Neurobiology at the Weizmann Institute of Science in Israel, revealed that certain circuits in the brain work on the same principle as FM radios, as reported in an article entitled "Tune In to This: Weizmann Institute Study Provides Evidence for a Radio-Like Mechanism in the Brain."[1] The article opened with these statements: "Research conducted at the Weizmann Institute of Science may give a whole new meaning to the phrase 'stay tuned.' Institute scientists

---

[1] wis-wander.weizmann.ac.il/life-sciences/tune-weizmann-institute-study-provides-evidence-radio-mechanism-brain

have found evidence that when the brain interprets sensory input, it uses a mechanism remarkably similar to that of an FM radio."

Frequency modulation (FM) receivers are tuned to specific frequencies or stations, and this frequency is continually altered or modulated. The FM radio receiver translates these modulations into different sounds. In the same manner, the brain appears to be tuned to its own "radio stations." Researchers at Radboud University Nijmegen in the Netherlands, in an article in *Neuron* magazine entitled "Brain Works like a Radio Receiver,"[2] theorize that the brain has a "tuning knob" that influences behavior. Their results suggest that brain circuits, like an FM radio receiver, could tune in to other frequencies.

These findings seemed to add credibility to the theory proposed by the messengers. Just as we use tuning knobs to adjust a radio's receiver to reach the frequency of a specific station, with practice our "tuning knobs" in the brain can establish and build neural pathways to make different connections to reach the same destinations.

May 1, 2014

This one has a thought how some of these messages have impacted the lives of the ones receiving them. When this one receives a message, it is done so by connecting her energy to the energy field that originated the message. Humans may refer to this connection as "awareness." When the message is received, it is in the form of an energy packet. The message consists of multiple energy frequencies that are received on multiple levels. Some levels are prominent; others are subtle.

The first level is awareness where the message—the words—are received. Awareness is energy. A stream or offshoot of energy comes from the home of the message to the energy field of the receiver. This stream flows from one energy system to another, connecting them.

---

[2] ru.nl/english/@930644/brain-works-like/

As I received this message, I envisioned a glass plasma ball with a mass in its center that glowed and pulsated. Offshoots of electrical current that resembled a miniature lightning storm spiraled upward from the core and arced toward a hand that rested on top of the glass ball, literally depicting the offshoot of energy the messenger had described.

When energy is streamed into awareness, along with it comes a fuller set of vibrational frequencies than just words. That awareness channel becomes part of the receiver's energy system as it alters the energy field.

Once the energy has flowed into the receiver's awareness, the melding and blending of the two energy systems result in a change of perception. It is understandable why this one finds changes in life, for it is not just the words, but the connection to the energy source that accompanies the message. These changes can be profound, for it is not just the receiving of the words, but the entire source energy associated with the words.

The *"fuller set of vibrational frequencies of energy than just the words"* referred to the scenes that played in the back of my mind with increasing frequency, even when I reviewed months-old messages. I realized this was no different from the increased awareness we experience with significant events. For example, most people can recall in full detail the events surrounding them on September 11, 2001.

When messages are received, energy streams are formed. Humans refer to this energy connection as "awareness." As more energy is channeled and exchanged between the source and the receiver, the channel becomes wider, allowing more energy to flow. Yet the energy goes both ways, but that is a topic of discussion for another time. Not only is the specific message entering the field, but also other energies that are associated with the message.

This is much like taking a bite of delicious chocolate. There is more to the exchange than what the taste buds register. It is the feel of the

21

chocolate in the hand. It is the feel of the chocolate in the mouth as it warms to the body temperature. It is the changing of the consistency of the chocolate to a softer form as it melts and spreads across the roof of the mouth and across the tongue, reaching even more taste buds. Now the sense of smell is engaged as a hint of cocoa reaches the olfactory nerves. As these events occur, the brain becomes engaged, responding to this pleasurable sensation by sending endorphins throughout the body. The rest of the body responds to these endorphins by reducing pain, relieving stress, and alleviating depression. There is more we could list with this example, but enough said.

Receiving a message from another energy system is more than just words; just as consuming chocolate is more than just the sense of taste. When this one receives a message, it is more than just words that are shared, but it is the entire energy from the connecting source of the message. Energy frequencies are received at a very subtle level but often not recognized. However, these energies do exist and it is these subtle energies, more than the words, that are responsible for life changes. It is this connectivity of awareness and surrounding awareness that is responsible for changing behavior. The message is more than just words.

Perceiving life through the filter of energy offered me a paradigm shift. As I assimilated this new information, I found myself viewing everything through energy, energy connections, and vibratory matches, and these new perspectives overshadowed my previous beliefs.

Almost a year after the initial discourse on neuroplasticity and the brain operating like an FM receiver, and after hundreds of messages on other topics, the messengers returned to these topics to offer a new analogy to describe energy connections. The new communiqués shifted from neuropaths to footpaths.

October 17, 2014

It is similar to walking through a tall field of wheat at night to a new destination. The first trek leaves a discernable path marked by footsteps that have bent and broken shafts of wheat. The return trip is easier, for the foundation for the path has been laid. Each trip widens the path, making it easier to traverse.

The same is true for connecting to other energy systems. Each connection is strengthened by the number of treks. Especially for those who are aware of these energy paths, the connection becomes even stronger and almost instantaneous.

A picture formed in my mind, and I saw myself standing on the outskirts of an enormous wheat field. The full moon's golden glow illuminated the wheat as it swayed in response to a cool breeze. I watched a path form by unseen steps crossing the field. My perspective changed, and it offered a bird's-eye view. From this newer angle, I understood how the initial trek created the foundation for connection and allowed easier passage for subsequent trips.

I began to notice a dwindling of the messages; several days would pass between them. As the frequency of the communications slowed, I wondered why. By this time, I knew I could ask for messages, but they seemed more genuine if spontaneously offered. As I questioned whether my connections to the messengers had ended, an answer arrived:

February 2, 2015

The initial messages this one received paved the way for different messengers. The initial connection was similar to a path a bulldozer makes when beginning to pave a road in a remote location. The connection was direct, yet somewhat rough. Now that the primary channel has been laid, the path has become smoother. The connection between this one and other dimensions was like a rough, knotted rope.

Now the connection is fine, like a silk thread. The connection is subtler, but the messages are more specific and definitive in nature.

Now that a channel has opened, there is room for subtler energies to trickle down to this one. This trickling-down of energy occurs almost nonstop. This one sometimes perceives what she thinks is a lull in the messages, yet this is not true. Much is happening behind the scenes. This one is becoming more capable of using her sense of expanded awareness to rise to meet those incoming energies. Instead of having specific messages, a general, overall connection has begun.

The physical and energy bodies of this one are changing. There are lessons to be learned, but more importantly, she is beginning to perceive things differently. There has always been a broad perspective, but it has been quite easy to remain stuck in the physical Earth plane, wrapped up in the drama of everyday life. We say now it is time for this one to ascend.

The time that this one perceives of as "quiet" has not been quiet at all. Indeed, it has been very active but on a subtle level. The process of allowing the energy body to expand and to learn to function from a broader perspective has begun.

This explained the reason behind my perceived lull in the messages. I needed time to assimilate the new energies and to adjust to the frequencies contained within them. Although I did not understand exactly what that meant, I felt it when it happened; something shifted. It is difficult to articulate, but I had reached a tipping point, and I had crossed some sort of invisible threshold.

As part of this shift, I had a mind-set change, and I began to frame my daily events in terms of energy exchanges. I thought of energy, how it worked, and the role it played in the foundation for not just the messages, but everything in life. I recalled Nikola Tesla's quote: "If you want to find the secrets of the universe, think in terms of energy, frequency, and vibration." Energy is the power behind the thrust of a rocket as it blasts into space. It is also the power behind the tiny bud on a plant as it bursts forth into a beautiful flower. It is everywhere. It is everything.

I received a download of information accompanied by a vision that clarified energy connections between senders and receivers: I saw a refrigerator's electric cord move toward a wall outlet. I heard a click as the cord inserted into the outlet, followed by humming from the refrigerator. The sender-receiver connection continued as long as the refrigerator remained plugged into the wall outlet.

In the next scene, I saw myself in the vision with streams of energy exiting my body, connecting to the energy frequency of the messages. The energy flowed as it had with the refrigerator. Should I lose the connection, I could again plug into the frequencies, and the energy would return to its previous flow.

I understood the connection between sender and receiver, but I often wondered, why me? I felt surprised to receive the answer: vibrational match. It is not solely the energy flow but also the vibrational match. Everything is energy, not only things but actions and thoughts. I received messages when there was a vibrational match between my energy field and the energy fields of the senders.

Often, we perceive ourselves as physical bodies that enable us to interact with our environment. But our dense physical bodies are only temporary shells; our true essence is nonphysical. Some call this energy; others call it spirit or soul. While on the Earth, we are spirits having a human experience.

Our physical senses help us to interact with our surroundings, yet this is just an exchange of energy. What we see, touch, taste, hear, and smell are frequency patterns that are translated into understandable data by the brain. When you bite into a ripe peach, sensors in your hands, eyes, mouth, and nose send information to your brain for interpretation. In that energy exchange, you learn about the characteristics of the peach. Does it feel soft or firm? Is its outside texture smooth or rough? Does it smell fresh or rancid? Does it taste sweet or bitter?

We use our hearing and our voices to communicate, yet communication begins with the unique energy vibrations of individual speech sounds that travel to the brain for interpretation and then understanding.

I started to recognize the many energy connections in our physical bodies. The lesson continued below, shifting from a download to the dictation method:

Thoughts are energy. Emotions are energy. The exchange that occurs between humans having a conversation is energy. There is nothing upon your Earth plane that is not energy, for humans are vibrational beings, and everything around them are vibrations. Plants, animals, and minerals have energy exchanges with each other and with Mother Earth. There are symbiotic energy relationships with all energy forms on the Earth plane.

It is this energy connection through which this one is able to connect to us. There is a vibrational match with us and a connection to our energy fields. As she continues connecting with us, those connections, those energy pathways, strengthen much like neural pathways that strengthen in the human brain with repetitive tasks. We have been on the outside of this one's field of awareness for many years. We have been able to connect through the dream state on multiple occasions. That connection is not necessary now, for the vibrational match has occurred in her waking state.

The messengers expanded my knowledge of the role of energy. It is not merely the foundation for communication, but the entire basis for existence. Humans are vibrational beings, and it is through the matching of energy frequencies that we connect to everything physical and nonphysical.

I wanted more information about energy as well as my connections to the messengers, so I set that intention. Within seconds, I learned about the energy prerequisites required for all communications, including messengers from beyond. To open channels of communication, letting go and allowing must occur.

It is the letting go and allowing that is the required foundation for channeling. This one has known this requirement for many years but has only begun to embrace it. Letting go and allowing with no expectations tied to the outcome is when the magic occurs. In humans, it is not only the brain that is the receiver of informational energy exchanges, but it is the entire surrounding energy field. It is as important to feel something as it is to think, see, or hear it. It is the use of the human senses, not in the limited manner in which most humans use them, but to expand the awareness in each of these sense organs in order to gain receptivity on an energy level.

Often humans can be sitting or standing by themselves, and for no discernable reason, they turn to see someone has entered the room. This is an example of allowing informational energy systems to become aware of another presence by sensing input from the surrounding energy field. They did not hear, see, feel, smell, or taste the new presence in the room, yet they became aware of this new person on a subtle energy level within the energy field.

Animals do this all the time, and it is labeled instinct. Instinct is the fine-tuning of physical senses so to increase their receptivity to changes in the surrounding energy fields. This occurred with elephants during the Great Tsunami in 2004. They went to higher ground long before humans were aware of impending danger. Most humans did not perceive the danger before it occurred. On an extreme level, this is what we referred to several days ago as the "butterfly effect." When a butterfly flaps its wings, it can be felt around the world. Because there is no such thing as empty space, one change in the surrounding energy force field affects the adjoining force field, and another, and another.

As Mother Earth continues her transition, more people will be sensitized to their surrounding energy fields. They will be able to sense activity impinging on the energy fields surrounding their bodies, improving their reception. As reception improves, the next phase is to ascertain changes in the intensity of energy beyond the force field next to their body, and so forth.

Letting go and allowing with no concern about the outcome and no expectation of results is needed to establish and maintain connection to areas beyond the physical body—a valuable lesson. Embrace it. For now, we leave you with this message.

This message may have addressed how to achieve a vibrational match, but it resulted in more questions. As I tried to assimilate the information about vibrational beings, other questions arose, questions about instinct, butterfly effect, extending our physical senses, and Earth's transition.

From an evolutionary perspective, people will become aware of energy fields and as a result, be able to sense things beyond the five physical senses. Everything is energy, and we are important variables in the energy exchanges occurring in that environment. Not only are these energy interactions part of who we are, but they also play a major role in Earth's evolution.

I had been given a lot of information to process, and I felt the foundational beliefs of my life shift and expand. Were my brain and my body simply mechanical features, like cogs in a grandfather's clock? I wanted more information on vibrational matches and energy exchanges. The answer arrived, seemingly out of nowhere: through energy packets that respond to our beck and call.

The information had arrived in the middle of a December night in the form of a download. It was Wednesday and time to turn in for a good night's sleep: 8:30 p.m. It's always early bedtime on Wednesday nights because I'm scheduled at a high school on Thursday mornings. High schools start early, so that means the alarm is set before 5:00 a.m. in order for me to be ready to leave my house by 6:10 a.m.

A few minutes before the alarm was set to ring, I woke up with the answers. Energy packets exist within structures similar to cumulus clouds. They float within these clouds and exist as pure potential until a thought, desire, prayer, or intention is set. The new desire sets a chain of events in motion that causes the cloud's energy components to shift in order to match the desired outcome. As other intentions arise, the energy packets split and recombine with other components to create different effects to match the new intentions. With each new prayer or intention, the newly combined packets drift to the forefront of the cloud to assume a direct position for contact with the person or people who set the intention.

The messengers' explanation seemed logical, and it clarified the premise behind the law of attraction and the importance of holding and maintaining prayers and intentions. As soon as you doubt the outcome of your prayer, wish, or intention, the energy packets split and rearrange to match the vibration of the newest intention—the intention of doubt.

In July 2014, I was attending a program at The Monroe Institute in Virginia, when I suddenly woke at 4:44 a.m. with an urgency to write. I grabbed for the notebook and pen that I had put on the bedside table before I had gone to sleep, and as fast as I could, wrote the following words that were bursting forth:

July 6, 2014

The essence or spirit of your greater self is magnificent. It is huge, wonderful, and expansive. The energy of your spirit, your essence, is too powerful to fully inhabit the human body. In order for this spirit to operate within a human body, the power/energy must be decreased. The physical body operates as a transformer does for electricity, decreasing voltage to a safer level.

The transformer qualities of the body reminded me of the radio-station characteristics of the brain. The description of our magnificent essence or spirit seemed to compensate for these sterile pictures painted of the brain and body. I wanted to hear more.

Eons ago our kind dropped physical form. We realized the physical form limited us in too many ways. Once our kind got a taste of our true essence, there was no going back to the old form. Why walk or take a bus across the countryside when thoughts can transport you in an instant?

Physical form fosters the false belief of separation. Now without form, we operate in Truth, for we are all one. We are energy. There are various energy systems or components which combine to produce specific effects. We can also be in multiple "places" at one "time." We put these words in quotes for there is no such thing as a place or a time. We are all one. We are all. We are everywhere. We are nowhere. We are now-here. It is all the same.

I did not know who these messengers were, but dropping their physical forms piqued my interest and brought me closer to the outer fringes of normalcy. In the past, I had thought physical senses measured reality, but that no longer seemed clear. If the body and brain primarily operated to house the true self, then were the physical senses just the gears in the machine? What was real? How do we know if we are on a path of truth?

I searched older journal entries for answers, and I found a six-month-old post about the validating role that signs play in guiding us on a path of wisdom. Asking for and receiving signs help us to trust the information received through nonphysical senses. Below is the older post:

December 15, 2013

Everything is energy, and easy to manipulate. When you are on the right path, we will bring signs such as multiple numbers. It is easy to bring a sign or message on the computer, radio, TV, or anything electronic. It is simply a matter of converting energy to the desired pattern.

These signs are used as minor guideposts along the way to indicate the energy frequency is in alignment with Source. Asking for signs brings the energy of intention to the forefront, clearing the path for the intentions to manifest.

I continued to receive information on topics too numerous to include in this book. But now and then an older conversation would resume even though months may have passed since the initial message. If I had not documented my exchanges, I probably would have missed this pattern because the half-finished conversations were interspersed and hidden among numerous other unrelated messages.

This intermittent arrangement of fragmented exchanges became apparent as I began to write this chapter. It was odd. These ongoing correspondences—although sometimes months apart—were seamless in content, as if they belonged with the initial conversations.

Why, and why was this phenomenon so apparent in this chapter and not elsewhere in the book? As I pondered these questions, messages began to flow into my awareness. This chapter introduced the concept of the brain operating like a radio tuner, and how I could learn to fine-tune my reception to receive specific frequencies. I realized this experience was part of a lesson meant for me:

January 24, 2018

As this one connects to a specific energy frequency, that connection is recognized by the brain. It leaves an electromagnetic marker that identifies the connection. This one has received information months apart because she reconnected to the initial energy frequency. The frequency is always there, and it operates much like a live streaming platform; it is ongoing information. It is always available, yet the information starts and stops in response to the connection to the receiver. When this one reconnects to the original source, the message continues as if it had never stopped.

As she learns to fine-tune her reception, there will be more clarity in the messages. They will no longer be intermittent, but more sequential, making it easier for comprehension.

It began to make sense to me. Just as FM receivers modulate to maintain connections to specific radio stations, I could maintain connections to frequencies by learning to recognize the individual electromagnetic markers of different energy systems. This is the fine-tuning referenced in earlier messages; that is what links and maintains the connections.

I was on my summer vacation, thoroughly enjoying my time off work. Summer in South Florida can be stifling hot midday, so I tried to take advantage of the cooler morning temperatures. I was on an early morning beach walk when a message arrived. I turned on my phone and recorded the following:

June 16, 2014

Most humans believe the five physical senses are responsible for allowing humans to experience the world. What they do not realize is that by using these senses, the totality of what is around them is diminished because only a small portion of the world can be perceived through these limiting senses.

I thought sharper physical senses resulted in more accurate experiences. If vision or hearing failed, glasses or hearing aids could restore these senses to their optimal states and enable the person to experience the world in the fullest capacity. Yet this message indicated the five physical senses limited our ability to perceive the environment.

In states of expanded awareness, as in meditation or dream state, the human is able to perceive the world with greater depth and clarity. The physical body has many limitations, including those imposed by the brain. The brain functions as a dimmer switch to dull a bright light. It is through this filtering process that perceptions are processed by the physical senses. Because of these transducer characteristics, input is limited to the levels the physical senses can tolerate.

Due to the filtering (reducing) mechanism of the brain, some things do not make sense; they are beyond the capabilities of the senses to comprehend. Understanding occurs outside the physical senses in the realm of expanded awareness. Because it is beyond the capability of the senses, humans consider the event as "non-sense." Yet we say to you, these "non-senses" are the keys to understanding, for they exist beyond the limitations of the physical senses.

Like most people, I had relied on my senses from birth, and I had never considered them as limiting. Now the messengers tell me that truth is found through the "non-senses." The foundation for perception begins with the heart, not the brain or the senses. Shifting attention from the brain to the heart results in fuller, more authentic experiences that are aligned with truth. I had difficulty believing this until I realized this was how I received messages. The visions I "saw" were not through the physical sense of sight, nor did I "hear" words through the sense of hearing. This message began to make more sense to me.

If humans learned to perceive with the heart, they would be open to all of the phenomena that occur around them. A truer picture of the universe would emerge.

Much is like the energy or the Spirit of Music. Some humans will listen to a symphony and hear only the notes from the individual musical instruments. If humans use only the physical sense of hearing, they will perceive only the musical notes.

If humans would allow the music to flow through the heart centers, there would be a shift to a state of expanded awareness, which would allow for a fuller, richer experience than what the sense of hearing allows. The music carries the listener to a realm of expanded awareness where the energy of love allows emotional reactions to certain pieces of music.

The event of listening is expanded when experienced through the heart instead of the ear, and the human may find tears in the eye or experience other emotions. This transforms their current Point of Existence into an expanded state. The same is true for art. Perceiving art with the eyes offers a limited view rather than perceiving with the heart.

As humans learn to move beyond the physical senses to experience events, lives will be enriched. Using the heart as a mechanism to experience events will increase appreciation and gratitude. Appreciation and gratitude are higher vibrational frequencies, encouraging states of enlightenment. When perceived through the heart, vibrations of love, appreciation, and gratitude are higher than frequencies experienced by physical senses.

A human can pick a flower and place it in a vase of water, or by being mindful and using the heart center, choose a flower by experiencing its energy. The flower can be honored and appreciated by welcoming it into the home. Both events result in a flower in a vase in the home, but the energy of one event is very different from the other event. Choose wisely.

As the words ended, I saw myself in a vision that included these two scenarios. In the first scene, I picked a flower and put it in a vase of water in my house. My vision replayed in my mind, this time in slow motion and using my "non-senses."

I watched myself in the first scene. As I severed a flower from a plant, tremors of energy shot through the stalk of the plant and into the roots deep in the ground. While observing, I felt the painful reaction from the plant, yet the "me" in the scene was oblivious. When I got home, as I placed the flower in a vase of cold water, frenetic vibrations emanated from the stem where I had cut it, again traumatizing the flower as it reacted to the cold water in the sterile environment of the vase. Although the blossom looked beautiful, the entire process felt cruel, and tears filled my eyes as I watched myself within this vision.

The second vision played in my mind's eye with very different results. I bent down, caressed the leaves of the plant, and admired its beauty. It reacted to my touch like a cat that arches its back under a hand to beg for a rub. We had established a positive connection.

As I admired the flower, golden sparkles of energy streamed from my hands to produce a vibrant blanket that covered the plant. The plant responded to my touch by releasing a beautiful combination of pink and green waves of energy. These colorful vibrations mixed with the golden energy from my hands and created a third set of frequencies. The transmission of unspoken words occurred within this new set of frequencies: I wished to take a flower home so the beauty of the plant would remain with me. The plant understood and honored my request.

I watched this remarkable process unfold. The roots of the plant began to vibrate as energy deep within the Earth moved up to encompass the root ball, adding a layer of protection. The vibrations continued upward through the stalk and into the stem of the flower. When it reached the tip of the blossom, the energy flow made a 180-degree turn, looping back on its previous path. It continued to retreat before it stopped at the junction of the stem and stalk. I saw a zigzag of energy that sealed and protected this section of the stem as the plant volunteered to release a flower.

When the energy stopped, I gave my heartfelt thanks to the plant and snipped the flower. I lifted the flower and, with as much compassion and reverence as I could, I carried this precious package home. A wispy trail of pink and green energy followed me; the energy connection to the plant had not been severed. Like a loving mother who allows her children to leave home to experience the world, some energy ties can never be broken.

I prepared its new home. I placed the flower in the vase of room-temperature water, and I stepped back to admire its beauty. Brilliant rays of energy came from my heart to cover and protect this beautiful flower. My energy became part of the flower, and yet the flower remained part of the original plant.

The flower began to radiate a breathtaking colorful array of energy patterns; it lit the room and raised the vibration of everything surrounding it. As I watched this in my mind's eye, tears, again, formed in my eyes, but now these were tears of understanding and appreciation for the lessons I had learned. Because I had taken time to connect with the plant, and I had asked permission to take a flower, the plant had given itself to me, yet it had not severed the bond to its flower. The life-force energy of the plant had accompanied its flower after separation.

Seeing and sensing energy requires skills beyond what the physical senses can register, yet it adds depth, dimension, and, most important, understanding. We can literally see the universal connections between all living things, not just to other people but to life. Everything is energy: thoughts, emotions, interactions.

"Choose wisely" resounded in my head. I had learned this lesson about connectivity of life through the example of a flower. The intentions and actions of the person picking the flower resulted in very different outcomes. So often we go about our lives, oblivious to our surroundings. But as we begin to appreciate the energy connections to all life forms, we can make our choices and decisions in an intentional and mindful manner.

The visions of the flower reminded me of the first message I had received on my morning commute in August 2013, *"Let us all be flow-ers of energy,"* not just with ourselves but among all living things. My willingness to allow the messages to flow into my awareness without judgment kept me in alignment, and I opened to experiences that were beyond my wildest imagination. I had become a flow-er of energy, and the "good vibrations" of each message enriched my life. Where else would this journey lead?

CHAPTER 3: FATHER TIME

Have you ever experienced déjà vu? Scientists say it is an anomaly of memory, making us think we had previously experienced a current event. But I know otherwise. It is not a hiccup in the brain but a form of time travel, and a skill we can learn.

This next stop on my journey addressed time and how it works. The messengers did not identify themselves, but the communications lacked the lyrical language of The Muses Within. For reasons unknown to me, it seemed important that I learn about this enigmatic construct called time.

Why is time so subjective? It flies when I am enjoying myself, yet it seems to stop during a root canal. The older I become, the faster time passes. Time is more than what the clock or calendar measures, but what is it? The messengers offered me a new perspective that began with something called the Point of Existence or PoE.

Spring break had ended over a week ago, and I was back into the regular routine of going to bed early, waking up even earlier, and working most of the day. Naples' weather is close to ideal this time of year; it's not too hot, and the Gulf of Mexico seems to have endless onshore breezes, especially at night.

I had just come home from work and changed clothes. As I was pilfering through my freezer in hopes of finding something to eat, the following message came into my awareness. I closed the freezer door and turned on the computer to record the following:

April 7, 2014

Many humans think of themselves as their physical bodies, separate from others. Their self-awareness begins from a small point in the center of their physical bodies. We refer to this as the Point of Existence (PoE).

From an aerial view, when several humans interact, their PoEs resemble scurrying insects or moving dots. Most humans do not realize that PoEs exist within a field of energy, capable of expanding and overlapping with other energy fields.

In my mind's eye, I saw something similar to an air traffic controller's radar screen. I interpreted the map with surprising ease. In this detailed, complex, three-dimensional display, moving dots represented people as they rushed in different directions. As I focused on moving lines of dots that I had identified as vehicles, another layer of the map opened and allowed me to view each passenger's PoE. The map's three-dimensional aspect gave incredible detail; I could even distinguish between people walking up and down steps from those riding in elevators.

I marveled at the remarkable clarity, and I cannot begin to offer an explanation of how, but by this time I had become more comfortable with the uncomfortable. Each step of my journey pushed the boundaries of reality a little farther and made the unacceptable a little more acceptable. My eyes opened to other possibilities. Each new message, such as this one, represented a small, colorful piece of a mosaic, and I began to awaken to a larger truth. Once again, to keep the energy flowing, I did not judge what I received. This left the door open for more pieces of the mosaic to be revealed.

Next, take a broader perspective, and view each neighborhood as a dot or PoE on the map. As with humans, the PoE of gatherings is also enclosed within fields of energy. Pull farther away, and find the PoEs from larger gatherings, what humans call states, regions, countries, and continents.

In response to the message, my view changed and exposed larger sections of the map until I could see the PoE of a city. I saw clusters of dots as people gathered in public places. My perspective zoomed out until I could see lines on the map delineating states, countries, and continents. If I focused on an area, the map peeled back to reveal multiple layers below, enabling me to drill down to see the PoEs of individual people.

Next, view the PoE of the planets in your solar system. Take an even broader perspective and view the PoEs between galaxies. This pattern continues beyond the galactic level to areas beyond human comprehension.

The previous scene replayed but this time with an expanded field of energy around each PoE. This view showed the complex connections that exist in our world. Dots became circles, and an increasingly intricate pattern formed as they touched and blended. Circles overlapped as individuals met on sidewalks, as cars passed each other, and as neighborhoods merged with other neighborhoods. Cities, states, countries, and continents overlapped. As before, when I focused on a specific area, the map drilled down to the individual PoE level.

Let us now add the concept of time. There is an energy field surrounding each PoE, and it exists outside of what humans refer to as present time.

Self-awareness associated with the PoE is location-dependent. And although the single point of the PoE is often deep within the physical body, it has the ability to disengage and float into the surrounding field of the four-dimensional globe, thus altering the perception of time.

Humans often think of themselves as separate from the rest of their world. They think of themselves as their PoE; the PoEs are centers of their universe. But this is not true; they are not separate. They are simply unaware of their divine connection to all that is.

As the globes of awareness interact with others, connections can be seen. There is unity, a relationship to all things that exist, including all times that exist.

The vision within my mind replayed, but the flat circles transformed into translucent globes. There were bubbles within bubbles within bubbles everywhere, yet I could see how they connected. When I considered the element of timelessness within each globe, I saw how the past, present, and future of one PoE could influence the past, present, and future of other PoEs it contacted.

These concepts represent truth. Many humans think of their existence as separate dots drawn upon a map. They do not grasp the "globe-all" timeless connection with others.

The pun of *"globe-all"* did not escape me. I know everything has a PoE, not just people but plants, minerals, animals, and even elements. There are global connections, and these images helped me visualize the global impact we have on each other. But introducing the concept of time made it more difficult to understand. Although I could visualize how time could be influenced by watching the globes of existence interact, I did not understand how. More information arrived about a month later, and that added clarity.

In May 2014, I saw a series of diagrams that introduced a different perspective on time. The initial picture depicted my current understanding: time was linear, sequential, and moved from point A to point B. In my mind's eye, I saw small spheres (representing the PoEs) superimposed on a straight line. The progression of these circles represented the one-way route from one chronological event to another. This direct track through time was the same whether the PoE was the sun moving across the sky, the flow of sand in an hourglass, or a person traveling to Grandma's house—time marched forward.

The illustration became animated, and rolling, repeating sine waves replaced the straight line. The path of the PoE was no longer direct; the now-curvy wave just made the trip to Grandma's house longer.

This third visual rendition of time brought clarity. The timeline's transformation from straight to curvy to crimped waves had resulted in an expansion of the PoE, and that was the key to understanding the mechanism of time—expanded awareness. Expanded awareness occurred as the PoE detached from the center of the physical body and then took residence in the adjacent energy field. This disengagement altered the makeup of the energy components as the individual, isolated particle of the PoE expanded into a field of energy. In this state, it covered more of the timeline, creating a gateway beyond the present time. The past and future could now be accessed because time was no longer linear. It had become malleable and fluid.

Once I understood the correlation between states of expanded awareness and their effect on time, the diagram changed again. The expanded circles morphed into three-dimensional globes, resulting in even more dramatic combinations of multitudes of overlapping globes of existence.

Each globe began with a single particle, the PoE, located deep in the physical body near the heart. In this isolated and restricted form, the PoE exists in the present moment. But as awareness expands, time shifts, and the past as well as the future can be experienced. The farther self-awareness extends into the surrounding energy field, the more expansive the senses become, which results in awareness beyond what was possible with physical senses.

As we leave our comfortable centers, what defines us melts away. We realize our physical bodies are not who we are. Time no longer exists as it did before. The farther we travel from our centers, the more we are influenced by other overlapping globes of existence. We are no longer in a world of predictable outcomes, but instead we float in a realm of possibilities. We are free to choose experiences from our past or sometimes events that have yet to occur.

With an unexpected traumatic event, an unanticipated and often startling state of expanded awareness can occur. This can also happen with the *observers* of the incident. One of the schools where I work is a five-minute drive from a Publix grocery store. In the morning, I go online and order sandwiches for lunch from their deli, and coworker Denyse and I drive to pick them up. Recently, while we were returning from our Publix trip, we heard tires screeching, glass breaking, and the unmistakable metal-on-metal sound that could only mean one thing: a vehicle accident. We both looked in the direction of the sound, just in time to see two cars colliding. Luckily, no one was seriously injured, but we both noticed how time seemed to stand still. As the windshield of one car shattered, hundreds of pieces of glass seemed to explode upward in slow motion before falling back to the ground, like a gentle shower.

Because we had both noticed the time distortion, this gave me an opportunity to share with Denyse the information I had received about the relationship between rapid expansion of awareness and the perception of time. This incident had created a blast of energy directly into our confined Points of Existence, which resulted in an explosion of our PoEs from small particles into gigantic fields or spheres of awareness. It was interesting to note that we both experienced this temporal anomaly.

Our spheres of awareness floated among the multiple curves of the timeline. As the spheres increased in size, the likelihood that a nontemporal experience would occur—such as time standing still or moving in slow motion—also increased. "Clock time" was no longer the norm.

Some people report viewing their physical bodies from above during near-death experiences (NDEs). Now I understand the mechanism of this phenomenon. The experience caused the PoE to detonate, and it unhinged the center of awareness from within the physical body. As it catapulted into the outer limits of the surrounding energy field, it resulted in a bird's-eye view of the body below.

There are different degrees of expanded awareness in the NDE state, which result in diverse experiences. For example, reports of viewing the physical body from above are more common than accounts of traveling to other realms and interacting with nonphysical beings. There is direct correlation between the number of sine waves within the expanded PoE field and the transcendent nature of the encounter. The more sine waves contained in the expanded state of the PoE, the less a person is tethered to time and space, and, therefore, the more mystical the experience.

We are much more than our physical bodies. We are not those small moving dots on a map. We are multidimensional globes of existence with the ability to expand in all directions, interacting with many other globes of existence in many dimensions, including the dimension of time. We can expand our PoEs and open ourselves to other energy fields; this results in perception far beyond what our physical senses are able to register. By expanding our awareness, we shift the boundaries of present time and expand our consciousness to interact with others "out there."

There are many methods to expand consciousness or self-awareness. Luckily, an NDE is not a prerequisite. In the previous chapter, we learned how the Emotional Guidance System can raise the vibrations in the energy field to make the energy body less encumbered and lighter—ideal conditions for perceiving other energy systems. With a lighter energy field, it is easier to engage the Energy Recognition System to help identify specific energy patterns or frequencies.

These techniques help fine-tune our brain's ability to receive subtle frequencies. Once engaged, we begin to build an energy foundation to help secure future connections. Each subsequent interaction strengthens the energy pathways.

Now I could add another tool to my toolbox for consciousness exploration: using the PoE as a vehicle to reach subtle fields of energy. Once we reach our surrounding energy fields, we find ourselves immersed in a sea of higher vibrational energies. From there we can engage our natural "antennae" to explore specific energy systems.

Relaxation and meditation are often prerequisites to connect to subtler realms, but many people have difficulty quieting their minds. Repetitive thoughts can race through the brain like a hamster on a wheel that constantly moves but goes nowhere. The mental chatter constricts the energy field and prevents relaxation. How can we quiet our minds to escape the hold these thoughts have on us?

We can break the cycle of repetitive thoughts by moving them out of the brain and into the heart, where they will be within our conscious control. The heart can send these thoughts into the surrounding energy field where they can be released into a space beyond awareness. Their hold on us is relinquished, and our PoEs are free to engage in their natural states of expansion. We become receptive to non-ordinary influences, and we can expand our physical senses beyond their usual capabilities.

How do we move the mindless chatter from the brain to the heart? The answer is simple; it is based on this basic formula: energy follows thought, and action follows energy.

It begins with awareness of the mental chatter as it occurs. I had already learned that energy packets associated with thoughts would align to match vibrational frequencies of an intention as part of a formal call to action. So, becoming aware of these pesky thoughts would start the vibrational-match process, and the energy associated with these random thoughts would be in place, awaiting further instruction.

The next step is to take action by moving those pesky thoughts into the heart. Using the formula above, energy will follow any thoughts we conjure. In my mind's eye, I saw a large butterfly net pass through my head that literally cleared my mind of this obsessive, repetitive babble. A thick, dark blob filled the diaphanous netting. This disgusting material represented my obsessive thoughts.

The net moved to my chest and dumped its contents as it passed through my heart. Within moments, the energy of the thoughts transformed into thousands of transparent, miniature spheres that

44

bubbled out of my heart and drifted outside my field of awareness. They were freed, released—no more brain chatter.

Another scenario flashed into my mind, and I saw the repetitive thoughts stuffed in an elevator. As it moved down the spine and reached my heart, the doors opened to release its contents. From that point, I could use any imagery (bubbles, smoke, balloons, flying pieces of dust) to push the thoughts beyond my heart and into the surrounding energy field. I continued to push the transformed energy away from my conscious energy field until it disappeared.

I was fascinated to learn how to reach expanded consciousness by using the PoE, and once in that state, I saw how imagery became as effective as physical action was in the normal waking state. What fascinated me the most, however, was how states of expanded awareness affected time. Could I go back and re-experience my past? Would I want to do this?

On September 20, 2015, I dreamed about time. When I woke the next morning, I grabbed a cup of coffee and sat at the computer to record it in my journal while the details were fresh on my mind. The characters in the dream, especially their style of clothing, suggested this took place in the early 1900s. Two men faced each other. An older man handed an ornate, gold pocket watch and chain to a younger man. Although I do not know how I knew this, the watch held significant value; it was a priceless family heirloom.

I closed my online journal. Once recorded, these images slipped from my mind as I changed my focus to more demanding tasks: grocery shopping and starting the dreaded laundry to get ready for the next workweek. Three days later, the messengers offered an explanation of the dream:

September 23, 2015

Time, indeed, is being passed hand to hand by those who are ready to receive the timeless message "all is love and all is now." It is but a parlor trick, this concept of time. Humans have always loved parlor tricks—sleight of hand.

For now, Dear One, you will be living in the space of magic, for time does not exist. It is an energy that can be passed from human to human, just as a pocket watch can be passed from human to human. As your ascension process escalates, "parlor tricks" will, too. What humans thought was magic will be demonstrated as truth. There is no time. There is no separation. There is only love. There is only now. Nowhere is now-here.

This one has been given multiple messages about time and how it works on the Earth plane. We tell her now the "time" has come for the masses to move into the higher vibrational frequencies of the upper realms and begin to experience life as it was meant to be.

The shift is occurring; we feel the energy vibrations of Gaia [the living spirit of Mother Earth] as her transcendence unfolds. There are many lightworkers who have felt the pull and tug of these higher vibrations, shifting and uplifting the energy makeup, changing the DNA. These changes are necessary to accommodate new frequencies associated with the shift.

Oh, yes, things are happening now, and it is a time to rejoice and celebrate, for a great awakening is upon us, a shift in consciousness across the Earth. It is time for the masses to rise like a great phoenix bursting into flame, only to be reborn from the ashes from whence it came.

Is time a gift, a priceless heirloom of knowledge to be passed from one generation to the next? Time relates to our concept of who we are, so perhaps the gift is the recognition that we are timeless, part of the realm of all there is, magically existing in the past, present, and future. Time is not static; it is fluid, subjective. It is a "parlor trick" because it "does not exist."

Just as a grandfather's clock strikes on the hour, marking time to those nearby, we are called to "experience life as it was meant to be." Timeless messages have been shared with humankind across the globe. We are all one. "There is no separation." We are not separate points on a map; we are beings of expanded awareness, connected to all, across all dimensions, including the dimension of time—past, present, and future. We are not isolated islands afloat on the sea of life; rather, we are life itself.

CHAPTER 4: CHANGING PERSPECTIVES

A car had hydroplaned off a dark, rain-slick highway, leaving it stuck in the middle of a muddy field. They would need to call roadside assistance for help, and that meant they would miss their scheduled event. Everyone was upset, but if they could have seen what I saw, they would have felt much different.

I had an aerial view of the event, and my larger perspective allowed me to see the full picture. Around the next bend in the road, a bridge over a small river had been washed away by the storms. A warning barricade had also been dislodged, no longer visible. Had they continued on the dark, wet road, the results could have been disastrous.

I realized the impact of my changed perspective. Although the occupants of the car would miss their event, they were safe. What they considered a calamity turned out to be a blessing because it prevented what would have been a catastrophe had they continued. Too bad they did not know what I knew. Shifting our points of view allows for different interpretations of events. Our limited understandings are left behind when we can see the whole picture.

This vision came in response to a new set of messages. The lessons on energy and time ended, opening the door for more pragmatic advice that could improve day-to-day living. As part of the human experience, we have various challenges, whether they are physical, mental, spiritual, or emotional. I welcomed any and all help to overcome these hurdles.

I expected some of the lessons, such as the advice on how to balance stress or to understand the benefits of forgiveness. But I was surprised to receive guidance on the value of *negative* experiences. These newer messages shed a different light on stressors such as fear, anxiety, and personal drama by demonstrating how these experiences could help me live a more fulfilling and rewarding life. By changing my perspective, these liabilities could become assets that might grant me opportunities for growth.

The message began with a basic: how to ask for help.

April 9, 2014

It is always best to request guidance from the highest Source, for denser energy systems are also capable of guidance. The Point of Existence can be established from an energy system of a lower vibrational frequency than the one requesting guidance. This would lower the vibrations of the one making the request. This is similar to the lesson shared about setting intentions. Review that lesson, and you will see the intention sets cascades of energies in motion in order to match the vibrational frequency of the intention.

This interested me beyond just the content; I wondered why the messenger directed me to review a previous lesson. This confirmed my untested hypothesis that some of the communications had originated from the same messengers. Like returning to class after spring break, I had to shift gears to get back on the same page as the professor.

I got up from the couch where I had recorded the message, grabbed my morning coffee, and walked to turn on the computer. I searched my online document where I had faithfully recorded the messages and found the lesson the messengers had requested I review—a lesson on setting intentions and PoEs. Intention starts a chain of events that cause energy packets to shift, align, and recombine to form frequency matches to the new intention. This reminded me of the importance of shifting awareness away from the physical body and farther into the surrounding energy field.

According to this lesson, setting an intention while in a state of expanded awareness is best practice. When PoEs move away from our physical bodies, bands of energy overlap. By setting an intention for positive guidance while in this interactive field, we attract higher vibrational frequencies. Because we are closer to Source, we are in a better location to receive the best guidance possible.

Guidance occurs within the overlapping energy field of the one giving and the one receiving assistance. The energy of intention activates the PoEs between the giver and receiver. The PoEs become attracted to each other like magnets, and the center of the PoEs connect in the person's heart space.

As I read the previously recorded material from the computer screen and sipped my still-steaming coffee, a vision began. As these PoEs snapped together, I saw a three-dimensional bubble of energy expand outward as it first encompassed and then extended beyond the person's energy field. The person floated within this slow-moving sphere. Guidance seemed to occur like a small nudge that would align the person with the intentions designed for his or her highest good.

Questions came to mind: Do most people know they should request help from a higher power? What happens if help comes from a lower energy field? What if the information does not resonate with us? Can we stop it? How does that happen?

As these questions arose in my mind, the answers came. The energy from all guidance is subtle, gentle, and can be overridden as easily as popping a bubble. By turning attention away from that specific energy, the thoughts will drift from the person's field of awareness, thus allowing him or her to pursue more suitable options. It is a matter of changing perspectives, because shifting PoEs create different points of view.

We often say people do not see eye to eye when they do not agree on a subject. We need to change perspectives in order to view a situation through a different set of eyes. The expansion of our PoEs into states of expanded awareness elevates our energy frequencies. Our limited views drop away and are replaced with an interactive and expanded world of possibilities.

It was a Friday, right after work. I changed into shorts and started walking on the beach. Sunset was still a couple of hours away, and I had planned to be home and showered by then so I could hopefully get a glimpse of the green flash as the sun set.

I had not taken over ten steps on the beach when the following message arrived. It was time to get out the phone and record while I walked.

April 25, 2014

From an individual Point of Existence, one human may harbor unkind feelings toward another because of a perceived transgression, when in fact the root of the incident may not carry the energy of transgression. The "transgressor's" PoE is different, that is all. By changing the PoE and shifting awareness to a larger perspective, the human will rise above the incident. When shifting awareness to a larger perspective, the subsequent energies will shift to become aligned with truth. The individual, isolated PoE of the "offended" no longer exists.

Much like the vison I had seen with the car stuck in the mud, when a limited perspective is replaced with the larger picture, the truth is revealed, and everything changes.

When this shift, or rising-above, from an individual/isolated PoE to a broader perspective occurs, the energy associated with it is a lighter, higher vibration. Humans have referred to this process as "enlightenment."

Enlightenment, indeed, is a state of existence in which previous incidents become insignificant. An example of this occurs when a tragedy happens to a close friend or family member. Daily lives are disrupted by the incident, and often this disruption allows the human to reflect on patterns in daily life. A different perspective—a different PoE—frequently results. What might have been thought of as

51

significant is now seen as minor in the broad picture of life. From an energy perspective, this is easy to understand.

I had not considered a connection between enlightenment and expanded awareness, but it seemed logical. In the not-so-distant past, I had identified myself as my physical body and my reality as what my senses registered. I had seen myself in different roles: parent, friend, spouse, sibling, teacher, and student. There are other roles that we might play, whether we want to admit it or not: the role of victim, aggressor, preacher, saint, and so on. The more constricted our view of self, the easier it is to believe we *are* the role. By moving our PoEs from isolated positions, we can see life through larger lenses, and we begin to understand these are only roles. They are not who we are but simply a part we play.

When a tragedy befalls, the human's PoE and energy field are changed. The human is often flooded with energies of caring and compassion from others. These energies are of a higher vibration, thus expanding the PoE, and for a short time, the result is a degree of enlightenment. Daily occurrences which were bothersome are seen in a different light and are no longer troublesome, for they have literally risen above their isolated PoE.

I knew this to be true—although I had never heard it articulated in this manner. I know how my perspective changes when I am called to "crisis duty" when there is a death of a student or staff member. My heart opens as I help others who are grieving and in shock. But along with these painful and raw emotions, there is a glimmer of light; a feeling of hope rises as I witness the outpouring of compassion for the family of the one who had passed. I cannot help but review my own life and realize how quickly unexpected events can change lives forever. I come home exhausted yet with a sense of resolve that I will no longer allow minor events to bother me. I find myself ready to forgive and forget. Even if only temporarily, I have risen to a state of enlightenment.

We say that if humans would continue to connect with this higher Source and constantly expand their Points of Existence, their hearts would remain open. It is the opening of the heart that is responsible for "ease" in their lives, just as the closing of the heart is responsible for dis-ease.

The previous lessons on energy had demonstrated the connection between ease and dis-ease. Repeated blockages (dis-ease) in our energy bodies lay the foundation for disease to manifest. By becoming flow-ers of energy, we could maintain states of ease and equilibrium that would allow a natural flow of life's energy through us.

The key to maintaining life's flow is through keeping the heart opened. As we learn to live beyond our limited PoE, heart energy expands. We become part of the field of overlapping PoEs, and we begin to sense universal connections. We realize we are never alone; we are part of everything.

In this state of oneness, as our energy frequencies change to higher vibrations, we attract more of the same. We love, and we feel loved. We see things in a different light, and we appreciate our surroundings more than before because we are an integral part of all that is. We are open and receptive, willing to accept other perspectives as the next section on forgiveness demonstrates.

Forgiveness carries with it the energy of love. It is not love for the perceived "wrong-doer" but love toward the one who needs to forgive. If one does not forgive, there is a blockage of energy at the very source of wellness—the heart. If the human body's physical heart is blocked, there is a lack of appropriate blood flow throughout, and organs will suffer. The result is dis-ease because the organs will atrophy or decay due to the lack of blood flow.

The energy of the heart works in the same manner. When there is an energy blockage of the heart, as in the example of someone who needs to forgive, there is atrophy of the entire energy body, resulting in a dis-ease not only in the physical body but also in the primary source of wellness—the energy of the heart.

Many humans are given opportunities for growth on the Earth plane. Many lessons are learned the hard way. If life were easy, fewer lessons would be learned. One of the most valuable lessons to learn is forgiveness.

As this one heard many years ago, that has remained with her, not forgiving is similar to taking poison in hopes that the transgressor would die. We say that this statement is factual. Forgiveness evokes the energy of self-love.

Until reminded, I had forgotten that statement. The analogy is appropriate; by not forgiving, you impede your own progress. You are stuck in a quagmire, and you create blockages that prevent spiritual growth.

The energy of forgiveness breaks the blockages. Just as opened floodgates in a dam allow a river to return to a natural flow and seek its own course, forgiveness opens energy pathways and offers an invitation for life to get back on track.

Forgiving someone does not mean you agree with his or her behavior or even accept it, but instead you are willing to move beyond it. Forgiveness is for you, not the other person. It loosens those bonds that have imprisoned you; it initiates the healing process.

A few weeks later, I had another reminder to shift my PoE to help improve decision-making. Next year's work schedule needed my attention. Should I stay in my current assignment or request a different location? There were pros and cons to both positions. Without a moment's thought to use any of the information I had learned about guidance, changing perspectives, or even my training as a psychologist, I obsessed over the upcoming decision, and debated what to do.

May 7, 2014

This one is reviewing workplace situations for next year. We remind her to think in terms of the PoE. Do not operate from the primitive position within the body, for this position allows for feelings of isolation and feeling wronged by others. But instead, rise above that PoE, and become enlightened by the needs and concerns of others.

We tell this one to trust that universal decisions will be made in her best interest as she continues to allow wellness and gratitude into her heart. Positive emotions such as gratitude, love, and wellness will help open blockages by allowing "globe-all" awareness to expand into the fields of enlightenment, a higher vibration.

When you perceive yourself as the isolated, primitive PoE, you cannot see the entire picture. We tell this one to trust the process, and the process will guide her in a direction that will be most beneficial. It is not something to worry about because worry blocks energy. These are the best words of advice that we can share with this beloved one.

This message reminded me about trust. I did not need to dwell on the pros and cons of any decision. As long as I maintained a positive attitude, the universe would do the work. A higher power would set things in motion, and opportunities would flow to me in a perfect and balanced way. The only prerequisite: trust the process, be thankful for all the blessings I have, and things would work out. They did.

Although it is not unusual for images and visions to accompany messages, the imagery with the next part of this communication seemed bizarre even by my stretched standards. I wondered whether I should share the words, yet spare the imagery, or eliminate this next section of the message altogether from the book. I decided to include the entire message; it felt disingenuous not to do so. Little did I know that during the final steps of editing the book, I would receive information that validated this decision. But first let me share this unusual transmission.

I envisioned a picture of a simple two-dimensional model that looked like an upright ladder of overlapping circles. I immediately knew the circles represented Points of Existence. As my eyes moved from the bottom of the picture toward the top, I noticed a pattern: as each circle entered the one above it, the overlap increased. This continued until the two circles were in complete alignment, with one superimposed over the other.

As each circle entered the one above, I noticed the overlapped section of the breached circle resembled a smile. With each "rising above," the size of the "smile" increased, and this made *me* smile. As I admired the profound yet simple picture, these words entered my awareness, *"Every smile that you give propels you upward, toward enlightenment."*

I watched in amazement as I saw myself appear within this diagram. I was a miniature figure, grabbing each rung of the smile as I clambered upward. Like a mountain climber ascending to heights unknown, I traveled the path toward enlightenment one smile at a time. The message continued:

Not unlike stepping stones, this upward energy continues, allowing for more and more bliss to occur. This upward energy transition is the functional mechanism of enlightenment. As you smile, you put forth the energy of goodness which allows for more light to enter your realm of awareness, your PoE.

Not only does smiling build positive energy, but it's also contagious. When I walk on the beach, I smile at the people I pass, and they almost always return the smile. I can force myself to smile—but before long, it becomes genuine, and I feel warmth spread throughout my body as my energy field becomes lighter. My breath deepens, and the grin opens the door for more positive feelings to flow. Smiling brings good vibrations.

As each smile in the ladder of enlightenment became larger, I connected with positive vibrations that guided me even higher.

This energy pattern continues upward toward the energy of enlightenment until the smile becomes a full circle, becoming the next globe of awareness as the previous PoE is completely encompassed by the higher vibratory frequencies. The new PoE has encapsulated the previous PoE.

The messages and the images continued and described what I had just seen. It seemed so strange but also comical, as I watched this tiny caricature of me climb the smile-rungs of the ladder of enlightenment one PoE at a time. Because each circle of the ladder encompassed more of the one above it, it shortened the distance between the rungs, and made the climb progressively easier. When the final circle had aligned with the one above it, I experienced a sense of completion, unity, and wholeness.

When I thought the strange could not get any stranger, it did. As the two PoEs became one, my mini-me stopped, let go, and drifted in ultra-slow motion to move away from the ladder of enlightenment in the calm, methodical full-body rotation of an astronaut in deep space, floating in tranquility. As I detached from the ladder, the boundaries of my line-drawn body began to disappear, and I disintegrated. But how could this be? The real me remained: my soul, my spirit, my essence. I became both nothing and everything. I floated in the primordial sea of all that is.

I continued to drift in this deep, velvety void of quietude, and I melted even further until I became the light. The me I had known disappeared and was replaced with a self-identity of stillness and peace. Then it happened. Within a profound silence, I drifted into an abyss and sank deep in this unknown yet somehow familiar place. Within this muted void, this space that contained nothing and everything, a sound came forth and enveloped me. It was the deep echo of the word *Om*.

Yes, reaching enlightenment brings with it the energy associated with the chant of the holy word Om.

For every smile that you give, that energy reaches up to the next half-circle of your awareness, much like stepping stones. The farther you climb, the more aware you become, and the more bliss you feel. When you reach as high as you can, that smile becomes a full circle. This is the connection to Om, all having to do with the vibratory status.

Cold chills racked my body, confirming the significance of the message. What had begun with a small, cartoonlike character of me climbing a ladder of circles ended with a profound message as I melted into enlightenment, engulfed by the vibrations of the word *Om*.

I had heard of Om before and thought it had something to do with yoga—a topic I knew very little about. I had to know more. I was curious as to why Om played such a powerful part in this message. I searched online and found an article entitled "The Meaning of Om" by Valerie Reiss.[3] She reports Om has been referred to as "the sound of the universe." Om continues to be considered the most sacred mantra in Hinduism and Tibetan Buddhism. It is represented by a symbol as well as the mystical sound produced when it is chanted. The sound can "calm the nervous system" as well as gather and focus the mind. In another article entitled "What is the Meaning of OM?"[4] by Rachel Zelaya on Gaia.com, Zelaya reported, "The sound OM is a vibration from which all of the manifest universe emanates. Form and creation come from vibration. OM is the most elemental of vibrations. It is the sound of the void."

As I read that last sentence, I felt more cold chills. The sound of the void? I recalled my experience at the top of the ladder of enlightenment: I had dissolved into a deep, velvety abyss of everything and nothing. I had found myself afloat, drifting into this void, enveloped by the vibrations of the word *Om*. This research seemed to validate the messenger's statement that *"reaching enlightenment brings with it the energy associated with the chant of the holy word Om."*

The Muses Within had suggested including this message in the book, but I had doubted that decision. I had thought the content was too bizarre—mini-me swinging through hoops like a cartoon character and a ladder of enlightenment leading to nothing and everything. Having "Om vibrations" surround me like a blanket of peace and serenity? To be true to the theme of being a messenger, regardless of how uncomfortable the topic or how these silly images made me feel, I had felt honor-bound to include it. After my

---

[3] huffingtonpost.com/kripalu/meaning-of-om_b_4177447.html
[4] gaia.com/article/what-meaning-om

research on Om, a sense of awe and wonder replaced my embarrassment. The muses had been right, and I could not believe I had considered omitting this message.

A friend gave me a gift that offered another unexpected validation of this message. I had met Gayle at The Monroe Institute in Faber, Virginia, in July 2016. We were roommates at the OBE Intensive program led by William Buhlman, an acclaimed author and America's leading expert on self-initiated astral projections and out-of-body experiences (OBEs). I felt passionate about attending this popular workshop because I wanted to learn more about my own encounters. Were my visions related to out-of-body experiences? Could I learn how to self-initiate them the way Mr. Buhlman teaches people to induce OBEs? I wanted to learn more, and I thought this would be a great place to begin.

When I arrived, someone escorted me to my room, where I met my roommate, Gayle. I had hoped we would be compatible since we would be spending the next six days together. Because of the large number of international participants who attend programs at the institute, I was surprised to learn that Gayle lived in Tampa, less than 200 miles north of my home in Naples, Florida. Gayle and I shared personal stories throughout the program, and by the week's end, we had become good friends.

In January 2017, Gayle sent me a book by Rajiv Parti called *Dying to Wake Up*. Dr. Parti is an accomplished anesthesiologist whose life became transformed after having an extensive and profound near-death experience (NDE). I discovered common elements between his NDE and the ladder of enlightenment from my message.

During Dr. Parti's NDE, archangels Michael and Raphael escorted him to the top of a "ladder of enlightenment." At the top of the ladder, he saw a being of light who was later revealed to be Jesus.

One of the archangels stated that the top of the ladder "is like everything and nothing." As Dr. Parti approached the being of light at the top of the ladder, he heard a distant chant of Om. When he reached the being of light, the chant of Om became more distinct and opened the door for direct communication. As the light faded, Dr. Parti experienced a cosmic void, "the realm where there is no realm." He also described floating weightless like an astronaut.

The similarities between Dr. Parti's experiences and mine astounded me: the ladder of enlightenment, the feeling of being everything and nothing, the chanting of Om, a cosmic void, drifting like a weightless astronaut. Having these same elements reported by another professional not only validated my own experiences, but also confirmed the wisdom of The Muses Within's decision to include these messages in the book.

A couple of months later, I gained new insight about personal history and current drama. As a psychologist, I had clients who seemed to be stuck in cycles of self-destructive behaviors. Whether it was addiction, abuse, or anything else, many had difficulty breaking habits and routines. Although outsiders could see these harmful patterns, the clients were often unaware. It can be frustrating and painful to watch our friends, loved ones, or coworkers repeat these unhealthy behaviors, unable to break free. I saw the potential benefit of releasing personal history. It reduced drama, but would it also help free people from these unhealthy repetitive patterns?

July 8, 2014

Letting go of personal history will eliminate drama. Drama occurs when there is a perceived wrongdoing or perceived injury by another person or a group of people. If you no longer engage in past personal history, there is nothing to react to. Personal history has its own set of energy. If you drag it along, it will only hold you back. Drama has no beneficial results; it has a multiplicity of negative results.

Images began to form in my mind, and I saw myself standing in a large grassy field, wearing a bulky harness and backpack. Cords that streamed from the backpack connected to a parachute lying on the ground several feet behind me.

The wind began to blow. It caught the folds of the parachute and lifted it off the ground and yanked me backward. I leaned against the pull of the cords with all my strength, but the parachute continued its upward motion in response to the ever-increasing wind.

Just when I thought the parachute would lift me off the ground, one by one, the cords snapped and incrementally reduced the tension on my back, until I could move forward. I was released from the burden of the parachute when the last cord snapped. I felt euphoric. I no longer had to struggle. I was free.

This message, especially its accompanying vision, demonstrated how much the past can affect us. How can we move forward in life if we allow the constant tug and strain of our past dramas to burden us? By not releasing the past, we are in an endless loop of drama where the scenes remain constant, but the characters change. Nothing can instill drama in our lives as much as our past. We are the ones in control. We can choose to release the past or let it imprison us and fuel our current drama.

Personal drama is often accompanied by worry. A couple months later, the messengers told me how worry could offer a chance for growth and maybe even wisdom.

It was a Thursday morning, and I had been up since before 5:00. I was showered, dressed, and ready to walk out the door to drive to work. As I entered my car, coffee in hand, I turned on my phone's recorder in case a message came through. I fastened my seatbelt, and before I could even put the car in reverse, the following began:

September 19, 2014

Worry occurs when a certain event, thought, or emotion rises into awareness. That event, thought, or emotion continues to rise, giving the human an opportunity to reframe this event, thought, or emotion from a different perspective. It is an opportunity for growth; it is an opportunity for learning; it is an opportunity to view the event from a higher perspective, and thus transform the energy associated with the event into energy of a higher quality. Many thoughts, emotions, and events are the basis of worry and are fear-based and thus are of a lower quality vibration—much denser and heavier energy than is associated with higher vibrational states such as love, appreciation, and compassion. Worry is an opportunity for growth when viewed in this manner.

When you find yourself worrying about something, stop and give pause. Within that pause, realize the opportunity for growth. For worry, without revisiting and reframing that event, can block the energy field. Energy blockages can manifest as dis-ease, causing a variety of physical and emotional energy disturbances, until the blockage is cleared.

Learn to trust the broader perspective. Often events, thoughts, and emotions occur for a reason that is not clear now. With a greater perspective, those events, thoughts, and emotions take on different meanings. The key to changing the negative, dense energy of worry to positive energy is to trust and allow life to flow, thus allowing events to unfold in the manner in which they were meant to—all from a greater perspective.

Learning when and how to move my PoE to gain a different perspective proved to be a valuable lesson. When I felt stressed, I could pause and view things differently. The pause allowed me to make a choice, and I could act instead of reacting. This offered me a chance to change and grow so I could live my life with thoughtfulness, consideration, and mindfulness. Not only had I learned to reframe individual situations, but I was beginning to experience the cumulative effect as well. Each lesson helped me view my entire belief system through a different set of lenses. I hoped to evolve into a better and more understanding person.

The earlier vision of the car and the washed-out bridge accompanied this message on worry, but this time with more detail. I was back in that scene, observing the people, their rain-soaked clothes, the barricade that was swept to the side of the road. But more important than the added details, I remembered the impact the vision had previously had on me, and it was just as powerful this time.

A broader view of events can change everything. It expands our narrow points of view and offers glimpses into the larger picture. When we leave our limited perspectives behind, we begin to awaken to a world of possibilities.

When the "rerun" of this vision ended, I remembered another time in which a different perspective might have changed the outcome. It is almost petty in comparison to the scenario with the car and the washed-out bridge, but it does offer another example to bring the topic of changing perspectives to everyday living.

Several years ago, while in a line of stopped cars trying to exit a crowded parking lot, I found myself behind a supersized pickup truck that made my car look like a child's toy in comparison. A couple on my right got into their car and started the engine. I blared my horn when I saw the car's backup lights come on. How could they not see the enormous truck behind them? The driver slammed on the brakes and stopped the car. The driver understood why I had honked and waved as a gesture of appreciation.

The driver in front of me was oblivious to the near-accident involving his supersized truck, and from his limited perspective, my horn was a rude signal for him to move forward in this gridlocked line of vehicles. He responded by sticking his head out the window in order to look at me, which made this personal. With his eyes locked on mine and an angry scowl on his face, he thrust his middle finger in my direction.

This incident has stayed with me for years. I have always wondered what the truck driver would have thought of his behavior if he could have viewed things from my perspective. His limited view prevented him from seeing the full picture.

It is natural to respond to events from our own perspectives without pausing to consider the larger picture. I wondered how many times the roles had been reversed, and I had been the one blinded by limited perspectives. I recalled multiple occasions when drivers had tailgated then had passed my car in what I had deemed to be an unsafe manner.

I had seen these situations from my own limited viewpoint and not from the perspectives of the other drivers. Why were they in such a hurry? Were they rushing someone to the hospital? I had no way of knowing, but after the lesson on changing perspectives, I wondered whether something dire had caused their erratic driving. I now give these drivers the benefit of doubt, and I try to make it easier for them to pass me.

A few weeks later, I learned I did not have to look outside of myself for assistance; I could use my own Emotional Guidance System. This win-win situation felt empowering. The Emotional Guidance System could help me in many aspects of my life.

October 1, 2014
Humans have an Emotional Guidance System to help guide them with their actions and decisions. This is similar to what other animals have that is commonly referred to as instinct. This Emotional Guidance System allows what is often referred to as wisdom to take the helm in decision making. When there are emotions involved, this is an opportunity for growth. If it is fear-based emotion (fear, worry, anger, jealousy, etc.), then there is given an opportunity to pause to allow the event, thought, or emotion to be reframed and seen in a different light.

This resonated with me. Animals' instincts guide them in everything they do, but it seems that we do not acknowledge our instinctual nature, much less follow it. Human instincts are forgotten traits, discarded along the evolutionary path long ago. We do not recognize instincts as our second nature that can guide us.

How often do we ignore gut feelings about something, only to later discover the wisdom behind them? We get into a habit of using our brains instead of our hearts, where our instincts are housed. We analyze and overanalyze decisions and discount the importance of our instinctual nature. The Emotional Guidance System returns instinctual wisdom to us.

When you see something in a different light, it literally describes what happens when your perspective changes. The energy in the form of light becomes different. It changes and allows for a changed interpretation. If there is an emotion of love, compassion, or gratitude, this is an indicator the human is on the right path, the path that is supportive and indicative of the greater path in life.

When one is on the right path, the physical body gives a clue or sign, thus indicating the alignment is perfect. A human may have cold chills or experience tears of joy. A human may smile and feel uplifted. This is part of the Emotional Guidance System. The system also reacts physically to fear-based emotions: cramps in the stomach, gritting of teeth, headaches, racing of the heart, blood pressure rising, etc. All of these physical reactions are part of the Emotional Guidance System.

Each human has the ability to use the Emotional Guidance System like a GPS system when traveling in unknown territory. It is there to guide them to their final destination.

By engaging our Emotional Guidance System, we are prompted to trust our hearts, our gut feelings. We awaken our dormant instinctual traits. Why travel blindly when this self-empowering tool acts as a torch to light our way?

The messengers taught me a life lesson about four months later. Stress seems to be ever-present in our busy lives. We talk about it, and even measure the difficulty of a situation by how much stress it produces. Stress affects us not only emotionally but also physically. It upsets our equilibrium and triggers "fight or flight" responses as the brain releases hormonal rushes of adrenaline and cortisol in our bodies. The long-term effects of stress are linked to many disorders, including high blood pressure, cardiac problems, stroke, depression, and anxiety. I felt eager to change stress in my life from a negative to a positive.

This particular message probably arrived at this time because of the stress in my life. It was early Monday morning. The workweek had just begun, and I really wanted to stay in bed and sleep. The school district where I worked had recently distributed report cards.

This led to a post–report card panic, and the phone rang nonstop from concerned parents who were taken by surprise by their students' failing grades. These calls usually ended in requests for immediate evaluations for their children.

As I dragged myself out of bed, the following message streamed into my awareness while I was in the shower:

February 2, 2015

In the Earth plane, there is a lot of what humans refer to as stress. They work too hard at their jobs, and it is stressful. They lose that job, and it is stressful, although they had been stressed about that job before they lost it. They have a significant other and that relationship, too, is stressful. They lose their significant other, and they find stress there. It seems everything they do, they feel stressed.

We say it is time to release stress. It is time to release and reframe what was stressful. Humans need to let go of their hold on stress and learn to allow life-force energy to flow through them.

By releasing blockages, we give ourselves the gift of renewal, the gift of mindfulness, as we make choices to continue either the path of stress or the path of peace.

Do not get stuck in the mire of stress, but instead embrace the day-to-day life that has been offered to you. Be cognizant of what might feel like a blockage, something that might cause stress on your system.

Look to see where the blockage is. Where is the dis-ease? What are you holding back? What do you need to release? Do not confuse stress with life. Life is full of challenges, for if it were not so, then you would complain that your life was boring.

Their suggestion to *"not confuse stress with life"* offered another opportunity to reframe events so we could react differently. Reframing these stressors as challenges empowered me to step out of the role of victim and into the role of victor. The choice is mine and mine alone; everything depends on the perspective I choose to use.

Take a deep breath when presented with a challenge. Use that challenge to refocus on your own system to view your blockages, your dis-ease. Move through those challenges with an energy of a higher vibrational status. Love, gratitude, grace, honor, and trust are higher frequencies that will help counteract what you once referred to as stress. We say to breathe in those challenges and allow your higher self, your heart, to guide you in making decisions.

I liked the advice to take a deep breath when in a challenging situation. An attorney had given me the same suggestion as I prepared for my first court case over forty years ago. As a psychologist, people regarded me as the expert; they didn't know how intimidating that felt to me as a new professional, fresh out of graduate school. When testifying, the attorney suggested I take a breath before answering any question. I felt scared, but his instruction proved quite helpful.

Something enchanted and mystical happens within this meditative breath. Time stops for a brief moment and allows a disconnection. Within this short void, a space forms between the event and the reaction, and disrupts the pattern of stimulus and automatic response. Birthed from this created space, a chance for action, no longer reaction, arises. This action is focused and thoughtful. This contemplative act of taking a deep breath is the foundation to access trust and balance, and it offers us an opportunity for peace.

Another four months had passed, and while I continued to receive numerous communications on other topics, it was mid-June before I received another message relating to a change in perception. This one addressed learning how to trust the subtle cues behind guidance.

I had survived another school year, and I was relishing my summer vacation. This was *my* time, and I could spend it with my children and friends. My granddaughter, Lorelai, had just turned three. Often Cassie, Dan, and Lorelai would come over for a swim in the Gulf of Mexico or in the pool. Lorelai was old enough to start having sleepovers with her Nana. We had so much fun, but when she left, I usually crashed on the couch for a few hours. I had forgotten how much energy three-year-olds have.

It was also time to finalize my summer plans. This was the best time to visit my son, Phillip, and his wife, Kelly, in Nashville. I also needed to schedule another week-long program at The Monroe Institute in Virginia—so much to do, and all of it fun!

While sitting at my computer looking for airline tickets, I felt the familiar tug of a messenger, so I changed gears and opened my messages document and typed the following:

June 18, 2015

The energy of trust is similar to the scent of a flower, a blossom. If your eyes are closed and you smell night jasmine, you know that it is present—it is there. But how do you know? Do you see the scent? No. Do you hear the scent? No. Do you feel the scent? No. You sense it. The energy of its smell is very subtle, yet its presence confirms that night jasmine is nearby. There is an energy vibration associated with everything on the Earth plane—from human senses to thoughts to emotions. Delve into the subtle energy of trust by knowing the energy of guidance is within it.

This was a lesson on learning to trust the gentle guidance that surrounds us. This assistance may not be as obvious as we would like, but we can learn to recognize its subtle nature by how it makes our hearts sing. When that happens, I am going to make a concerted effort to quiet my mind so that I may hear these words of wisdom.

The summer came and went too quickly, and by the time September 2015 rolled around, my life seemed to be on overload. I did not feel stressed as much as busy, very busy. I had good intentions of working on the book, but other projects demanded my attention, and I wondered how I could get everything done. The following message arrived in response to my harried state:

September 4, 2015

The time will come when this one will drop back into that space where messages from The Muses Within can be heard. This is all about balance—the balancing of energies that are approaching. It is a balance and a choice. It is much like when given a plate with numerous food selections. A human may eat corn, for example, before the salad. It is all good, and it will all arrive in due time.

By wishing it to be otherwise, the human is creating a blockage which prevents what he or she wants to occur from happening. By stepping back and allowing the energies to flow in the manner and direction in which they are flowing from Source, then all is well.

Oftentimes, humans refer to a phrase, "too much on my plate," to symbolize the state when numerous energies have simultaneously approached their fields of awareness. We say it is not "too much on your plate," but instead a plethora of options from which to choose. Humans do not get upset and cause energy blockages when choosing a specific food to eat from an overfilled plate. Nor should they cause an energy blockage from tasks (in the form of energy), that approach them.

We say your perception of the approaching energies is what will result in either a neatly formed queue or a blockage. Think not of "too much on your plate," but instead, think of these energies as an overabundance of delicious offerings just waiting for you to choose what you wish. Instead, allow those choices to flow to you, and thus unfold in a manner of allowing. It is all there for your choosing. Think "My cup overfloweth" with abundance.

The power to reframe situations made me realize I could feel abundant instead of overwhelmed. When confronted with multiple phone calls and overlapping appointments at work, could I see these as opportunities to appreciate having a job? Could this be a chance to acknowledge that others value my opinions and seek my input? There are multiple ways to interpret events as positive instead of choosing to feel overwhelmed. It is up to me to decide how to react.

Allow energies to flow through you. When you stop in your field of awareness and spend time thinking about which option to pursue, what task to complete, you have just created a blockage.

When humans allow their egos to be the decision-makers, the plethora of choices becomes "too much on their plates." We say to go with the flow. We say acknowledge the abundance offered and be grateful, for those are the energies of allowing.

Recognize these energies as opportunities for development. When you acknowledge the presence of these energy choices, you are allowing them into your field of awareness. By continuing the energy of allowing, those energies will neatly rearrange and form a queue. This queue is in perfect order for you. These energies patiently await your recognition and full attention to them when you are ready.

We say that if humans would just abide by the previously espoused instructions to allow the energies to flow, then when the task is presented in order from the arranged queue, the time requirements (Earth plane terms) are adjusted. For the task is now being given to them in perfect order, allowing the energies to flow in a manner for which they were designed.

It begins with the breath. The flow begins within the space created by breathing. Make your breath purposeful, and it will allow for balance and equilibrium.

This reminder about the importance of flow brought back my memories of the first message from The Muses Within about the flow of the flower. Allowing this natural rhythm not only helps us, but can also assist others, as this next message suggests:

September 17, 2015

Many humans use the term "holding space" to refer to what they do when listening to another human or a group of humans who share stories of emotion. They hold space to keep that human or group of humans in supportive stillness.

Especially when the emotions of empathy and love are present, there is a natural tendency to connect with others from the heart center. When the heart center has made the connection, energy frequencies shift to become compatible with the other human or group of humans. Their energy patterns become stronger and more stable.

I had received many lessons that prepared me to live a more spiritual life. Some were easier to accept than others. I never blindly trusted them as truth but would take time to process the information. Sometimes the bizarre format of the messages, as with the mini-me scampering up the ladder of enlightenment, made it difficult to withhold judgment, but I felt determined to take whatever information came through and later decide if it resonated with me. I felt eager and curious to see what might happen next, so I kept the channel open.

A couple months after the lesson on holding space, the messengers shared practical advice on how to incorporate these teachings into my daily life. If we began each day from the authentic centers of our hearts, our paths would be cleared.

We often cause the detours we face; they are not due to other people. It is easy to get caught in vicious cycles of false beliefs that limit who we think we are and, therefore, restrict our choices in life. It is time for us to awaken to the divinity within and to find our authentic selves.

November 5, 2015

Every day when you awaken, you should live from your authentic center. You should go directly to the heart, for the heart is connected to the true self, the true nature of you. The authentic self is divine; it is centered, calm, peaceful, loving, and wise. It is a center of stillness and peace that resides within the heart of each human that lives upon the Earth.

There are some humans who have not awakened. Those humans do not operate from their authentic centers but instead from their egos. They take a circuitous path which will lead them away from the trueness of who they really are by these numerous detours. For when they do not begin each waking day from the center, from the true home, the path is not clear. These detours are reactions to false beliefs that were caused by the past, including past lives. There are deeds that the humans have interpreted as being painful or as injustices. There are lies that say the humans are not good enough; humans have been injured by words or deeds of others.

We say all of that is forgiven. We say all of that is false. We say those beliefs are only smoke and mirrors. All those beliefs create shadows that come between the human and the true path which starts at the home. These beliefs prevent the humans from seeing the truth. We say to get rid of those shadows. There is no karma; there is no need for karma. There is no need to put themselves in an energy field of anything other than perfection and divine order.

This powerful passage made me realize if our true selves are hidden, then so are our missions in life. We can change that. We can intentionally live from a place of higher energy, a place where peace, love, and gratitude become the norm, and that will grant us greater perspectives. We are the ones in charge of our lives. There is no need for karmic debt. We are not responsible for the sins of our past lives. We can start on new paths and right any wrongs. We can step out of the shadows of our limited belief systems and onto the lighted paths of truth.

We say that each morning upon awakening, be still, be silent. We say to return to your home where you are loved. Use the breath of stillness to tap into the energy of your home, your heart. Take a deep breath and breathe in the essence of your authentic self. Know that this is who you truly are. Throughout the day, as you find yourself drifting from this anchor of stillness and centeredness, we say to become aware and once again return to the heart center.

It is time to awaken to who you really are. It is time to forgive yourself of your beliefs about past mistakes, past errors, past shortcomings whether they occurred in this life or in past lives. It is time to forgive others who have, in your belief system, performed injustices against you. It is time to awaken your own eyes and turn those eyes inward to the truth of who you really are. This is a lesson that is being learned by many humans across this Earth as they awaken to their paths of authenticity.

So we say to you, each morning anchor yourself into your heart space. Go ye not into the world without guidance, for when you react to beliefs that do not stem from the true self, your circuitous path will be filled with detours, preventing arrival at the destination. But instead, begin each day from a solid anchor of divinity from within, and the path of your journey will be brighter, truer, and more direct.

Four days later while stopped at a traffic light on the way to work, I glanced out my car window and noticed a mature bald eagle regally perched on top of a light pole. I gazed at this magnificent bird and felt an overwhelming sense of gratitude that lifted my spirits. I realized I had been guided by my authentic self to see this beautiful sight. As I acknowledged my Emotional Guidance System operating within my heart, the following message began:

November 9, 2015

This is how guidance works; it is how it is. It is a nudge, a reminder. It is like a wind, a soft breeze that gently moves the blossoms of a flower in a field. It is gentle but ever-present for those who are willing to tune into the frequencies.

There is a gentle guidance that occurs with every human and everything upon this Earth. Animals live by this guidance; it is called instinct. Animals think not of what to do nor do they analyze their day, but instead they simply allow themselves to be guided to the appropriate paths. This is something a human can learn to do as well. It is a matter of stopping the wheels that are running in the head and instead, listening to the beat of the heart. It is within the frequency of the heart that true guidance originates.

We say it is time to take time. It is time to stop and no longer seek but allow; it is time to no longer think but to feel. In order to feel the gentle guidance that is present, take a deep breath. Take a deep breath from the center of your heart. As you take that deep breath, place a smile upon your face, for smiling brings forth the energy of gratitude and thankfulness. These are higher vibrational frequencies that will invite more guidance. It is as if your senses have improved; you begin to hear, see, and feel things that you did not before. Awareness is increased and along with awareness is the gentle message of guidance, nudging you upon the path that is right for you. By listening to the heart, you will learn the true meaning of guidance and how your nonphysical senses will be sharpened in order to hear the call.

I had once thought of stress and worry as negative yet natural by-products of life, but now I could see them as opportunities for growth. Energy exchanges, reframing events, mindfulness, heart-centered awareness, trust, learning how to forgive, recognizing and accepting gentle guidance—I had learned many lessons to help me live a more thoughtful, less judgmental life. How we handle ourselves during challenging times defines who we are. As we begin to recognize and reframe "negative" experiences, a little bit of grace is added to the formula for living.

Stress, personal drama, worry, and anxiety become positives when we understand that we are the ones in control. We can direct our energy to help others. We make choices, and through those choices, we set up energy exchanges that can either guide us to a more rewarding and fulfilling life or to a life filled with negative emotion. It is all a matter of how we frame these events. We have the power to change our perspectives. Will we?

CHAPTER 5: COSMIC CONTACTS

Years ago, I stepped outside my house and was stunned to find the ground covered with multicolored gemstone clusters. The scene looked like a rainbow version of Superman's fortress of solitude. Not only were the stones colorful, they were alive. Where was I? When I felt the warmth of the sun on my back, I looked up, hoping to see that familiar yellow ball blazing in a blue sky. What I saw surprised me.

Although unknown to me at the time, this dream represented a prelude to the next stop on my journey to the unknown—contact with cosmic beings. The October 18, 2013, dream was extremely vivid, and I was fully lucid, aware of my surroundings, actions, and thoughts. I felt alive in the dream. After I walked outside and saw the ground covered with gemstones, I looked up at the clear, cloudless sky to see the sun. Something had changed. There were two distinct shafts of light embedded in the sun's rays. As these new streams of light reached the precious stones, their multifaceted surfaces produced a spectacular display of colors that was almost blinding. It was as if the sun had brought these jewels to life.

I was curious about what I had seen. When, still within the dream, I woke the next morning, I stepped outside to gaze at the sun again. The divergent rays remained, but instead of two, there were seven specific beams. I felt even more curious.

In the dream I went to bed that night, but my anticipation kept me awake. Would the following day bring more changes? The next morning, I rushed outside and looked skyward. A complete metamorphosis had occurred. Although still a bright, fiery ball in the sky, the sun had transformed into a lotus flower with a thousand petals springing from its center. I knew these petals represented the rays of the sun. I had no explanation for the events, but the experience filled me with awe.

Even within the dream, I had wondered whether these events were real. Could others see this or just me? The dream shifted as if in response to my silent questions, and I gazed over my shoulder when I heard my neighbor's front door open. Her eyes were on the sky as she stepped outside. When she turned to me and asked if I had seen the sun, her question confirmed that the changes were real; I had not imagined them.

I had a "knowing" during the dream, similar to what sometimes occurs in the messages, and I knew the changes in the sun's rays were altering Earth's elements through the gemstones. I wondered why.

I recalled the dream in full detail when I woke the next morning. The sun's transformation into a lotus flower with a thousand petals puzzled me. Why a lotus flower, and why such a specific number of petals?

I found an article online entitled "What is the Thousand Petaled Lotus?" This lotus is said to represent the seventh or crown chakra.[5] (Chakras are swirling disks of energy located near the spine; the crown chakra is located at the top of the head.) The article reported that the thousand-petaled lotus is the most important chakra because it represents enlightenment, expanded consciousness, and the ultimate connection to the divine.

My dream of the lotus flower with a thousand petals defied logical explanation. I wondered how I could know things outside my personal experiences, but realized the information did not come from me, but through a dream. It must be a precursor to a message,

---

[5] blog.sivanaspirit.com/thousand-petaled-lotus

because it fit the pattern of receiving new information that would later be verified.

This new step in my spiritual journey kept me moving forward, but everything I had known stood still. Did truth remain behind, or did it reside in these uncanny shards of knowledge that I hoped would eventually complete the mosaic? I stayed true to my mantra: I remained willing to listen to more.

As soon as I woke the next morning, I went immediately to my computer to document the dream in my journal. Coffee would have to wait; this felt too important. But before I could type the dream entry, the following message arrived:

October 19, 2013

The sun is another source of its own. The energy emanating from the sun is powerful and divided into separate rays. The different rays from the sun represent different levels and types of energy. That energy goes throughout the universe to the areas where those particular frequencies are needed. There are humans on the Earth plane who can recognize the separate energies and are able to channel them to where they will be of greatest benefit.

The last sentence puzzled me. I recognized the different rays, but only in the dream state. Would I be able to channel the sun's energies to help others? Would that also occur in the dream state? Are actions in dreams practice for waking consciousness?

Of concern to us is the energy of Mother Earth herself, for she has been fighting an uphill battle. Humans have not realized her importance, and what they do to her is also affecting them. There is a disconnect between humans and Mother Earth. We have changed the energies we give your sun in order to give Mother Earth a more intense experience. We are able to fill the gaps created by mankind's misuse and overuse of Mother Earth's resources.

The subject of global warming is an example of the *"disconnect between humans and Mother Earth."* Global warming is an interesting yet controversial subject; some believe it to be a hoax while others are just as adamant that it is an undeniable fact. From the perspective of the messenger, Earth needed healing, and this was accomplished through a change in the sun's energy.

There is a new type of lightworker on the Earth who is able to gather these subtle energies and send them deep into the core of Mother Earth for healing. These lightworkers are beacons, drawing specific subtle frequencies into their personal energy fields, and then releasing the energies deep into the Earth. These are specific energy frequencies targeted for healing your beloved Mother Earth.

Just as crystals store and amplify energy in our three-dimensional world, so did the gemstone clusters in the dream. They operated as magnets that attracted the energy from the divergent rays. When the rays struck their surfaces, they infused them with a new set of energy frequencies that caused them to awaken and come to life.

Each gemstone has specific healing properties. The divergent rays activated these innate elements which resulted in a multitude of restorative energies. When the energy signature of each cluster mixed with the frequencies of the divergent rays, thousands of healing combinations resulted. The stones stored this new energy and magnified it before releasing it deep into the heart of Earth.

It is with sad realization that we must do this for Mother Earth. She is ever thankful for all the help we give her. It is an effort between some humans and our energy system working together to give the needed assistance. As humans evolve and are able to accept within their bodies a different type of energy, this new energy from the sun will be instrumental in healing other humans as well as Mother Earth.

Earth is addressed as a sentient being, as alive as we are and capable of receiving healing energy and also giving thanks. I felt reassured to know help was offered. The message continued:

This new energy brings with it a higher level of healing and more specificity. With it is the ability to heal dis-ease. What the human race calls miracles will occur more frequently. As lightworkers begin to use these newer energies, combined with the energies they possess, all will benefit. An energy loop of healing frequencies is established, benefiting all. Yes, as Mother Earth heals, humans will heal. Mother Earth is bombarded with these different rays of energy from the sun source creating a vibratory rate change to a finer and subtler energy. This is part of what your kind refers to as the shift.

I had heard of the shift before but only incidentally. This section brought the shift to the forefront of my awareness.

Mother Earth is shifting and rising to a different energy frequency. She can no longer be sustained in the energy field which she now possesses. It is with love and deep concern that we offer and send a different set of vibrational frequencies to her, differentiating the energy waves to her which in turn change the vibrational frequencies sent to humans.

This shift is gradual. This is a small step, but more are forthcoming. As she shifts her energy, the frequencies of the entire Earth plane change. The energy of rocks, trees, and plants will shift. Humans will become more open and will be able to communicate with elementals [fairies, gnomes, et al.].

Humans will begin to have an awareness of what your kind refers to as fairy folk or other-dimensional beings. They have been here for a long time, always helping Mother Earth in her journey. At an earlier time, humans were in tune with them and did, indeed, communicate with them. Now most humans think of fairies as fantasy, and they do not believe they are real. Fairy folk are coming back into awareness because the energy we are now giving you from the sun source is an energy in which they thrive. Welcome this energy field that will help the human race.

This was definitely one of those times I would have preferred to alter the words I received. But similar to the earlier entry with the mini-me climbing the ladder of enlightenment, it felt disingenuous to delete it, so here it is—fairy folk. But, I had to remind myself of my mantra to withhold judgment and just receive the information.

Many humans think nothing exists unless it is registered by the senses. When they meet face-to-face with elementals or other-dimensional beings, their belief systems will be severely challenged. They will question everything they have learned. This total shock to their belief systems will force another shift on an individual level. This will cause a differential energy vibrational shift to occur, which will result in their centers of existence shifting from their brains to their heart centers. This is the beginning of inspiration, for their connection to spirit has begun.

All will be well. We are making sure of that. With love and peace for now, appreciate and welcome this new energy. Good-bye.

Although difficult for me to withhold judgment about fairies and gnomes, I could relate to the section about challenged belief systems. It had happened with me. I remembered how shocked I had felt when I received the first message. I had no frame of reference. By not judging the content (because I was too stunned to do anything else), the messages had drifted into my awareness. As the information continued to flow, the boundaries of my reality stretched to limits I had not thought possible.

We can feel and sense energy by using nonphysical senses. With that comes the realization that we are much more than our physical bodies. Expanding our abilities to experience the world beyond what our senses measure will cause a shift in consciousness. We will know we are a part of everything; we are not just isolated human beings. If we could see the energy connections with others, would that not change everything? We would see other points of view. We could replace animosity with understanding. Peace would abound.

I had a lot of information to consider, and it all started with a dream. This new communication ended with hope and reassurance that all would be well. The content and the closing remarks were different than anything I had received before; new messengers had arrived. This aroused my curiosity. Who were they? Where were they from? True to form, the answers to my unspoken questions arrived the next day.

October 20, 2013

The question you ask is where we are from. Where we are from is not important to us, but it is to you. We are from a system that oversees many of the stars including the star in the Earth plane that you refer to as the sun. She is one of ours, and we can direct our energy to help change her vibratory signature.

We originate from a place that humankind refers to as Alpha Centauri. We have made connections with the Earth plane multiple times over millennia. It is now during this time when Mother Earth requires help with her transition that we are able to connect with others such as you.

What? I knew nothing about Alpha Centauri. I almost wanted the message to end, so I could search it online.

There are others such as you who receive messages from us. Of key importance is what you do with these messages. Our primary purpose of contacting humans such as you is to aid Mother Earth in her transition.

Some people may refer to us as extraterrestrial; however, that is not an accurate descriptor of who or what we are. We are an intelligent system or species of energy, just as all humans are systems of energy. We do not have separate bodies like are seen on the Earth plane. But instead, we are able to collect our energies for a common goal. We combine into groups for specific purposes. Each of us can leave a group to join another group of energy to which we are called.

Our goal is to help; our purpose is pure. We use our collective vibrations to manipulate and change the vibratory status of the objects upon which we work. This change in vibratory status is required for healing. This healing is needed for Mother Earth.

Alpha Centauri? The starship *Enterprise* could reach it using their warp drive in the television series *Star Trek*—that was the extent of my knowledge of Alpha Centauri. I needed to broaden my understanding, so I checked several Internet sites. I learned that Alpha Centauri is the third brightest star in the sky and the closest star system to our sun.[6] One of its stars is larger than and half-again as luminous as our sun, and it is located in one of the largest groups of stars in the heavens, the Centaurus constellation.

I could hardly believe what I read, but it all fit. It made sense for our sun to receive energy from the closest star system, and one with a larger and brighter star than our sun. I could not have made this up, even if I had tried.

The next day I received a message from Chiron, who turned out to be another celestial friend. Although I had never seen or heard the word "Chiron," I knew its spelling and pronunciation. In my mind's eye, I saw the printed word "Chiron" with "/k/" written below it.

October 21, 2013

Several knowns have been given to this one:

- *We are a system of energy, and we gather for a common purpose, a common goal.*
- *We are unlike humans. Humans perceive themselves as individual units; we do not.*
- *We have the recognition we are all one, yet we can bring specific energy frequencies together and become stronger and more powerful with a common purpose.*
- *We gather together for a common goal, quite often with the purpose of healing.*
- *As our goals are accomplished, we divide and are attracted to other groups or gatherings for the purpose of focusing on another target.*

It was given to this one this morning the name of Chiron. In humankind, the word "chi" represents life-force energy. This is a

---

[6] earthsky.org/brightest-stars/alpha-centauri-is-the-nearest-bright-star

descriptor of what we do. We gather together for a purpose to combine our energies to give life force to those in need. This is what we are doing to Mother Earth, and she welcomes our energies.

I had never heard of Chiron, so I did an Internet search. I could only shake my head in disbelief when I learned a celestial object named Chiron actually existed. Like Alpha Centauri, Chiron is also associated with the stars; it orbits the sun between the asteroid belt between Mars and Jupiter and the Kuiper Belt beyond Neptune. From the NASA website, I learned that Chiron was the first of several new hybrids found in space.[7] These new objects do not conform to any one known designation; they share aspects of comets, planets, and asteroids.

Messages from Alpha Centauri followed by Chiron? I had to learn more, so I searched a little deeper into the background of these new cosmic relations. With this second round of research on NASA's website, I discovered the name of this new class of objects: Centaurs, named after the half human, half horse mythical creatures. In Greek mythology, Chiron was the name of the wisest and most nurturing of the Centaurs, the tutor of Achilles and Hercules.

The centaur connection to Chiron sparked my interest about the centaur connection to Alpha Centauri. What were the details behind the obvious name connection? Alpha Centauri is part of the Centaurus constellation, named so after the centaur called Centaurus. In Greek lore, Centaurus was reported to be the father of the entire race of the mythological hybrids called centaurs.

The centaur connections from Chiron to Alpha Centauri fascinated me. The day after Alpha Centauri contacted me, a centaur communicated with me—Chiron. What was the relationship between these two cosmic messengers? Perhaps the meaning would be found in the remaining message from Chiron:

---

[7] https://nssdc.gsfc.nasa.gov/planetary/factsheet/chironfact.html

We have given these energies directly to our sister star, what you refer to as your sun. Your sun's rays have changed. There are seven new levels of energy that have not been present in the past. These new rays are needed in Mother Earth's transition. These rays will jump-start her into a new phase of being. This new phase is one of purity, clarity, hope, and health. As she moves through her transition, she brings the human race along with her.

Three days after I had dreamed there were seven divergent rays in the sun, the messengers described seven new levels of energy contained within the rays—all designed to help the Earth heal and transition to a new phase of being.

There are those such as this one, this human, who will be instrumental in gathering these energies and helping humankind in the transition. Make no mistake, whether there are humans helping in the transition or not, the transition will occur. As Mother Earth ascends, her humans must also. The transition will become more obvious when humans are aware.

Humans will become confronted with challenges they have never had before. Do not be afraid, for these are not challenges of cataclysmic origin as many humans have feared.

A brief online search revealed the belief that we are in the middle of a shift. It began with what some call "The Great Shift of 2012," that infamous December 21, 2012, date when the Mayan calendar ended. A lot of media hype surrounded this date that instilled fear that the world would come to an end. It even inspired a mega-disaster movie, entitled *2012*, that depicted the Earth's destruction by various catastrophic events. The movie painted an extremely bleak future.

Because my birthday is December 21, each time I heard the date, it piqued my interest. It seemed impossible to ignore the melodrama surrounding that date, yet December 21, 2012, passed, and the Earth still stood. The end of the Mayan calendar did not equal the end of the world, and Earth's survival gave rise to a more balanced view of the shift. The shift no longer meant annihilation. Quite the contrary—it represented a means of self-preservation for the spirit or soul and a transition to a more spiritual realm. The shift became a process of ascension to the fifth dimension, where the consciousness of love, compassion, peace, and spiritual wisdom abide. There would be a spiritual awakening, and people would expand their consciousness to step into their multidimensional existence.

The BBC News reported that the end of the Mayan calendar represented the beginning of a "transformation of our consciousness."[8] Daniel Pinchbeck, author of *2012: The Year of the Mayan Prophecy*, called December 21, 2012, the "hinge point" of the arrival of a more enlightened age, its entrance ushered in by the Northern Hemisphere's winter solstice, which brought us days with more light—a literal renewal of light. Perhaps this light had already begun its infusion into our energy fields.

The message continued:

As we have mentioned before, with these transitions, humans will begin to see and experience realms of existence that have not been visible in the recent past. Sit back and enjoy this as it happens. For those of you who are enlightened—that is, those of you with finer and subtler energy frequencies—will see this as amusing. You will find the old regime will become confused. They will no longer have upon their minds the making of money on Wall Street, for their entire belief systems will crumble. Again, enjoy the process as these people begin to see elementals [fairies and gnomes]. Your psychiatrists will have what you call a heyday. These people know what they see is true. They will be forced to move their centers of power from their head spaces to their heart spaces. This is all part of the transition as Mother Earth moves forward.

It is for now that we end this conversation with blessings.

---

[8] bbc.com/news/magazine-20764906

Oh, no. Once again, they tell me the fairies will make themselves known. That would certainly catapult individuals from their current belief systems.

This prediction took an unexpected turn almost three years later.

In June 2016, long after I had received this message, I met Fatima from Brazil at a residential program at The Monroe Institute in Virginia. During a dinner break, she told me about a friend who had photographed a fairy. As I listened to her story, my thoughts returned to these messages that predicted fairy folk would make their presence known.

Fatima's physician's husband had captured a digital image of the fairy while at a remote camping lodge in Brazil. Fatima showed me her picture of this photograph. I saw small branches floating on a rippled surface of a lake. Muted shades of blues, yellows, and browns dappled the water's surface as it mirrored colors of the sky, sun, and surrounding foliage. I could see the reflection of a large tree, its bark riddled with cracks as its sinewy trunk reached toward the sky.

The photographer soon discovered he had captured more than just the tranquility and serenity of nature. When he returned home and enlarged his digital images, something caught his attention: a tiny figure resting on a small branch arching over the water's edge. This figure looked like an attractive young woman in pale green clothing with shoulder-length light brown hair. But her diminutive size and wings suggested she was anything but ordinary. As I looked at Fatima's picture, I could see the fairy's face, arms, and light blue wings that faded to off-white near the tips.

As Fatima shared the story and her copy of the photograph (which is unavailable for publication), my mind returned to the prophetic message about fairy folk that would make themselves known. That message surprised me, but I never expected to have it validated almost three years later.

These synchronistic findings kept me interested, and I wanted to hear more from cosmic beings. I did not have long to wait. The following message arrived the next day:

October 22, 2013

Your sun has seven new sets of rays. Within each ray are seven different levels of frequencies. Humans refer to this as "seventh heaven," for seven times seven represents the greatest level of frequency vibration there is, at least in Earth terms.

The seven subsets within each ray act as a bridge to connect each frequency to the next. At the top of the frequency band, these vibratory energies arc to the next ray. If one were to see this as we can, it is a sight to behold. There is beauty and symmetry especially when the vibrations are perfect matches for its intended subject, our beloved sister — your sun.

This message contained several references to the number seven. I was certain that the seven new sets of rays referred to the sun's seven divergent rays I had seen in the dream. There were also seven levels of frequencies contained within each ray. What is it about seven? Why is it such an important number?

The information about seventh heaven also interested me, so I did a quick online search and found a site revealing that seven celestial bodies are visible in the heavens from Earth (the moon, the sun, Mercury, Venus, Mars, Jupiter, and Saturn).[9] Could this be the connection to the seventh heaven?

Several religions refer to seventh heaven in their doctrines. Both Judaism and Islam suggest the seventh heaven is composed of divine light, and Jesus is described as being surrounded by divine light, according to *The Church of England Quarterly Review, Vol XLIV*. This seemed to support the messenger's description of seven times seven representing the *"greatest level of frequency and vibration that there is."*

---

[9] earthsky.org/astronomy-essentials/visible-planets-tonight

As Mother Earth soaks up these rays—yes, just as humankind soaks up sunshine—the spaces and gaps are healed. These gaps are more than blockages; they are depletions of vibrant life force.

It is the life-force energy of your sun that radiates life. The radiation is through the act of shining. It is through life-force shining, life-force giving, that the sun is able to provide Mother Earth with the required elements for healing.

Seven is considered a magical number, just as when the seven colors of the rainbow are present, humans can see them. The number seven is the perfect combination for change. When it is multiplied by seven, it is the ultimate for effecting change. This is the makeup of the new rays we have given our sister star.

These rays have given and will continue to give Mother Earth what she needs for her ultimate healing and transition to the next level. It is our responsibility to oversee all our sister stars. We have come together at other points in time to heal other stars. The Earth has always been important to us as we watch and learn from her humans who appear so blind. They are all one unit, for life is all one, but they do not see this. This amuses us that humans think of themselves as separate from Source as well as being separate from each other.

This suggested a long-standing tradition of the messengers overseeing other stars in addition to our sun. I was taken by surprise to learn of the value and importance that Earth has had for them and how the messengers had learned from us, especially with our limited, isolated perspectives.

Each ray has a life or a vibrancy of its own. What humankind thinks of as life is a very limited point of view. Life is where life force is. Life force is everywhere. Most humans would perceive of life in plants and trees but would not think of life in rocks or boulders. The life force is within all, for all are frequencies, and frequencies are energy. They are all the same.

The message was clear. Life force was everywhere, not just in the obvious places like mammals, fish, fowl, or even plants, but in minerals as well. Life was related to energy. If there was an energy frequency, there was life. Although a new concept for me, it seemed to make sense.

These rays from your sun are teeming with life. Each of the seven rays will give Mother Earth what she needs where she has been depleted by humankind. These rays will patch her and give her what is lacking. As she reaches a new level of wholeness, her life force will change as she ascends to subtler realms. This is when humankind will begin to see changes in their lives. What was once a rare occurrence will become commonplace. These are the miracles that we referenced.

Rays that send help to specific areas of depletion sounded like an enhanced form of targeted infusion therapy, but rays *"teeming with life"* suggested the elixir was alive. Did the crystalline clusters in my dream serve this purpose? Each type of crystal possesses a different healing characteristic. As the divergent rays shined on each crystal, its specific healing properties came to life, just like an elixir *"teeming with life."* Did the combination of crystals and divergent rays in my dream infuse new life into the depleted areas on Earth?

These rays are different types of life force than what most humans understand. These rays will give Mother Earth what she needs as your sun shines those new rays on her.

As referenced earlier, when combined in units of seven, a separate life force awakens. When combining the seven times seven, another level of awareness opens. This is what is needed for Mother Earth, and this is what she is being given by us by way of our sister star, your sun. It is the ultimate in which we know how to send and change. It will create an arc of energy that will become an energy pathway for Mother Earth to follow as she begins her transition to wholeness.

The frequencies come from our sister star because this is a previously established connection for her. We are not able to send our energies directly to Mother Earth. Our frequency levels are too different and cannot combine or meld with hers. The frequencies must be sent to a source already connected to Mother Earth. We are sending this new energy to the sun, but we also gather together to effect change on other planes of existence.

For now, we prepare to leave you, as you say, for the day.

Rays that are *"teeming with life"* and those that are a *"different type of life force than what most humans can understand"*? Although I couldn't begin to translate what this meant as far as the type of help Earth received from these rays, the information comforted me. Since Earth had welcomed these healing energies, I figured we should, too. The Earth is going through a shift, an awakening to a larger consciousness, one of spiritual growth and renewal. The best news was that we are not alone; galactic friends have gathered to help us.

I continued to receive daily messages but not from my cosmic friends. It seemed they had stepped aside to make room for other messengers. Over the months, I had learned I could reestablish contact by simply setting an intention to do so. About three months later, I decided to check in with my galactic gang.

January 29, 2014

You asked about the star connection, and we are here, as always, in the background, awaiting your request for contact. We are the group that has been instrumental in opening the channel for this one. We are the overseers of the energies affecting Mother Earth, and we have a direct impact on what you call the interface, that way station or space between dimensions. We use our energies to help alter the energy of our sister star (your sun) in order to help Mother Earth in her transitory process.

Energy is everywhere. It is entertaining to see humans who think space is empty, for there is nothing empty about space. Humans who use only their physical senses are missing out on magical realms available through energy connections and energy intent. We are pleased when we see humans recognizing and engaging in nonphysical energy and energy patterns on conscious levels of awareness. Many humans who are not able, or perhaps not willing, to acknowledge the existence of space that is not empty, are missing enriched experiences.

I felt happy to reconnect with my star friends. Again, I heard the reminder to consciously engage the nonphysical senses to interact with the environment. It is through these non-senses that we can expand our awareness into the spaces that most of us think are empty. Fine-tuning our nonphysical senses allows a glimpse into worlds others do not recognize. It expands our horizons and allows us to see the bigger picture.

As Mother Earth continues her transition, more humans will be aware of these energy connections, and it will become commonplace for them to rely on those connections on an everyday basis. This is an assignment that has been embraced by many lightworkers, including the Dreamers.
So, yes, we are always here, just awaiting a request from you.

I wondered who the *"Dreamers"* were, but I supposed I would find out when they were ready to tell me. My understanding of the messages indicated that there is a synergetic relationship between the changes in Earth and the changes in everything that dwells on the Earth. As Mother Earth's frequencies change, those new frequencies affect all her inhabitants.

This relationship becomes cyclical. As people experience spiritual transformations, the more cognizant they will be of their universal connections to everything. They will begin to experience the energy of what they thought of as empty space, thus verifying universal connections to all that is. The more adept we become with these skills, the more we help Earth, not just our individual selves.

I enjoyed hearing from my cosmic friends. Over time, I had grown accustomed to several messengers who communicated with me, and I recognized their energy and life force. Each messenger presented with unique energy. When I reconnect with them, it seems like a homecoming or an unexpected encounter with a close friend.

Although the communications with these specific messengers had dwindled, their words were profound and remained with me for a long time. I always knew the messengers were still "out there" somewhere, overseeing and protecting Earth and all her inhabitants. The cosmic connections faded into the background of my awareness and made room for other messengers.

It was Friday night, and I was relaxing while I planned my weekend activities. I had been organizing my various online journals when I realized it had been about fifteen months since I had heard from these cosmic messengers. It was past time for another reunion. I decided to check the status of Earth's transition, so I tossed my request into the ethers of the universe. That query served as an invitation, and the following message arrived:

May 8, 2015

Yes, she is evolving and has "turned a corner" since the tipping point on 12-21-2012. She is on an upward path, leaving the past behind. This is not an event, but a process. The direction of her path has changed. During this time of transition, Gaia is receiving help from us and other star systems.

I recognized the energy signature when the message began, but I questioned one change. The word "Gaia" had replaced "Mother Earth." Merriam-Webster's online dictionary revealed another mythos connection: Greek folklore described Gaia as the ancestral mother of life who presided over all the Earth. Moving from "Mother Earth" to "Gaia" reflected the spiritual nature of the shift and identified December 21, 2012, as a tipping point in Earth's evolution. It seemed we had passed a critical point.

As we have told this one in the past, we have aided our sister star in providing Gaia with much needed help. We have helped to change the vibratory frequencies of your sun so those energy waves reaching Gaia will help her heal. There are many things humans refer to as negative that need to be changed. We do not say they are negative, but instead, energy frequencies of lower vibrations that need to be changed. The changed vibrations are beginning to nurture Gaia, just as the morning dew begins to quell the thirst of a dry day on Earth.

I liked the statement that negative events are just *"energy frequencies of lower vibrations that need to be changed."* Not only did the wording offer a less emotional perspective, but also it suggested solutions, solutions that were already in process, as the next section of the message shows:

As Gaia transcends from lower vibrations to higher frequencies, so will her inhabitants, including humans, plants, and animals. There are other finer attunements being made to Gaia, but those changes cannot be seen as much as felt. As her vibratory nature becomes further attuned to the higher frequencies, those invisible energy waves will penetrate the atmosphere and the inhabitants.

For example, a plant may become healthier. However, if humans could see or perceive the energy field around the plant, they would see why the plant is healthier. The plant's vital energy force—those energy frequencies specific to that plant—has increased. The same is true for all inhabitants of Gaia from rocks, mountains, streams, oceans, fish, and fowl to all animals, including humans. As Gaia strengthens as she heals, the energy vibrations of her inhabitants also strengthen.

What might have been perceived as dark or murky auras or energy fields are becoming cleaner and clearer. As the lower vibrational frequencies are replaced with higher-energy vibrations, the life-force fields surrounding all elements begin to shine and grow. It radiates forth and becomes a guiding light. Like attracts like; there will be others finding those who radiate at the same frequencies.

Had I witnessed this in the dream, when the crystalline clusters came to life as the divergent rays shined on them? Had their lower vibrational frequencies been replaced with higher ones?

This pattern will continue to increase until humans will be able to tap into a stream of consciousness where all thoughts will manifest. Manifestation will become instantaneous when this occurs. This is the direction Gaia is headed. Instant manifestation occurs in some realms; it is not magical, just a natural by-product of the higher vibrational status of its inhabitants. Gaia is progressing, but in Earth terms it will take time for this to occur.

A silent vision accompanied the message. I saw two magnificent blue-green Earths drift toward each other within the velvety, starless void of deep space. The two Earths met and began to overlap. The movement stopped when they were in perfect alignment that created one magnificent Earth. This new Earth represented more than both blue-green planets combined.

I zoomed closer to see the landscape, and as I passed over oceans, lakes, and rivers, crystal-clear waters came into view. I saw breathtaking waterfalls, and I flew close enough to feel their spray as the waters plunged into deep blue pools below. I soared over jungles, deserts, mountains, and plains. Plant and animal life were healthy and abundant. All the colors of this new Earth were brilliant and vibrant. I saw perfection. This new Earth had come to life. Tears came to my eyes as I watched this magnificent process unfold. Could this be the future, or did it represent the past before we upset the delicate balance in nature? I realized I no longer saw Earth as a blue-green planet in the Milky Way Galaxy but a living spirit. I had witnessed the transition of Earth—the birthing of the spirit Gaia.

This had a profound effect on me. These celestial messages comforted me as I realized we were never alone, ever. The messages required time for me to process, but I learned to view everything through a different set of lenses. Life surrounded me. I saw plants, animals, and now planets and stars as sentient beings, as much alive as people. I felt humbled and honored to be a recipient of these communications.

I heard again from my celestial friends, but the next message came as a surprise. In August 2016, while searching for a specific voice memo on my phone, I discovered an untitled recording. I hit the Play button, curious about this fifteen-month-old entry. What had I recorded? The voice on the recording was choppy and unfamiliar. I listened for almost one minute before I realized it was my own voice. These voice changes were indicators that a new messenger had arrived.

December 17, 2015

There will be a full moon on December 25th. The moon represents feminine energy, feminine frequencies from Source. There were celestial indicators guiding many to the birth of the man known to you as Jesus. The celebration of that event on December 25th coincides with the full moon. The full moon represents the greatest aspect of feminine energy. It sends forth love, compassion. Upon this most holy day, there is the celebration of the great ascended master, Jesus of Nazareth. He is the representation of love and compassion.

A virgin birth—Christmas Day would certainly qualify as a celebration of one of the greatest aspects of feminine energy. My online search confirmed the full moon on December 25, 2015, and it was the first Christmas full moon in thirty-four years. The next Christmas full moon would be in 2034.

We are blanketing this Earth with a different set of energy frequencies, resulting in a manifestation of those higher vibratory frequencies such as love, compassion, gratitude. Our energies are strong. Our energies are powerful. Our energies will be felt by many upon this Earth plane and will be instrumental in effecting change.

This celestial object's ability to blanket the Earth with powerful energies implied a *direct* energy connection. This represented a significant change, because earlier messages indicated the energies from Chiron and Alpha Centauri were too powerful and different for direct connections to Earth. The changes made through Chiron and Alpha Centauri required an intermediary—our sun.

Our energies are associated with lunar energies for we are a reflection, a direct reflection, of the brilliant star of Source. We were the guiding light that was seen at the birth of the Great One. We are that brilliant star of Source, for Source gave forth of its energies so the Earth might have peace, love, and compassion through the birth of the Great One.

I could not believe what I heard: a *"brilliant star of Source"* bringing *"peace, love, and compassion through the birth of the Great One."* This *"guiding light"* had to be the Star of Bethlehem. The Star of Bethlehem gently blanketed our Earth with the higher-energy vibrations of love and compassion. But I still wondered how those energy vibrations could do that without going through another source like our sun. The answer arrived on Christmas Eve.

December 24, 2015

There is an influx of new frequencies that are reaching your Earth plane. It is due to various protections set forth by your galactic brothers and sisters that allow inhabitants of the Earth plane to absorb and tolerate these energies without damage.

These energies are like water on your Earth plane; water seeks its own level. These energies are attuned to those on the Earth plane who are ready to incorporate those frequencies into their existent pattern of vibratory frequency. The energy does not affect those who are not ready to receive.

We are aware this is a time of love and gratitude that is celebrated. Because of this, we are able to reach more humans than usual. It is their alignment with higher vibratory frequencies that results in an openness to receive these frequencies. Many may associate our energy with the energy of ascended masters and angels. Although this is not totally true, we see the truth in these interpretations. For we come to you in a time of what many humans see as discord. We come to those who have love in their hearts and who have been touched by the Angel of Peace that is so honored upon Earth during this holiday season.

We are honored to be part of the New Earth as she awakens to become the brilliant star she is.

Twenty-six months before this communication, the energies of Chiron and Alpha Centauri had been deemed too strong for direct contact with Earth. Not so now. There are new energy frequencies from our *"galactic brothers and sisters,"* that suggested more and different energy doors had opened. Had the sun's rays initiated this new process? Had they paved the way for these newer energies?

Through this direct contact with Earth, these newer frequencies began to affect the people who were able to receive them and bypassed those who were not. Contact with higher vibrational frequencies encouraged more of the same, so I found it no accident that these energies arrived in December, the time when many Jewish, Christian, and Buddhist people celebrated significant religious events that were filled with appreciation, compassion, love, and thoughtfulness.

What began with a message about a flower had morphed into communications from galactic messengers. At times, it was difficult for me to believe these events, but message by message the journey stretched the boundaries of my belief system in a steady, progressive way that made it easier to accept. The messengers from Chiron, Alpha Centauri, and other interstellar emissaries certainly added an adventurous element on my expedition into the unknown.

My next encounter would be even more intense and personal.

I attended a meditation in August 2016 that ended with an unexpected turn of events. I received the following message moments before the event began:

August 2, 2016

It is all about the flow and the balance, Dear One. We work to balance the energies in all dimensions, but we hope you receive the balance within your heart.

As I wrote these words in my journal, I felt energy shift throughout my body, and I saw myself in my mind's eye. I watched as a shaft of light passed through one side of my rib cage, through my heart, and out the other side. As bizarre as that sounds, it did not hurt; in fact, it felt powerful, grounding, and even soothing.

The bar of light extended about eighteen inches beyond both sides of my rib cage. The light made a sharp turn and moved upward until both ends connected about a foot above my head. When the two shafts of light joined, I was enclosed in a triangle of light from my head to my chest. I felt a sense of completion, unity, and power.

My vision shifted to a three-dimensional mode, and the triangle morphed into a pyramid of light. As the message continued, I experienced three of me: one writing in the journal, one encased in the pyramid of light, and one observing the other two.

It is the tipping point, this most sacred balancing point of life. It is the heart that leads us. It is through our hearts that we have balance in order to flow through life's challenges. Embrace this feeling. Live this feeling. Be at one with this feeling. Be at peace with this feeling.

I felt a stream of energy begin to seep down from inside the apex of the pyramid. It began at the top of my head and trickled slowly down my body. The corresponding vibrations covered my forehead, eyes, and jaw. The movement stopped at my throat where the energy collected in what I can only describe as an energy puddle.

Something surfaced from the pool of energy that startled me and rendered me speechless: a being of light. This being of light introduced himself/herself by name: Zahur from the Pleiades. The message began:

You are correct; I am a being of light. I do not inhabit physical form. I come from the Pleiades. I am the communicator for the group, much like a spokesperson.

Over the years I had learned to respect the content of many of the messages because subsequent research of the material indicated it was true. And although I had seen many internal pictures and videos, I had never seen a being until now. In October 2013, the messages stated that people would become aware of fairies or other-dimensional beings, and almost three years later I had heard Fatima's story. Two months after seeing Fatima's photograph of the fairy, this face-to-face visit with an "other-dimensional" individual occurred.

I saw an egg-shaped ball of light form in front of me in my mind's eye. Golden sparks in the bubble of light coalesced and began to take a humanoid shape. The message had indicated they did not have bodies, so the shape was probably a means to provide some level of familiarity or comfort for me.

Zahur had light, wavy hair that fell just above the shoulders. The being had large round eyes but no discernable mouth. I got the impression there were other beings within this oval-shaped sphere of light, but Zahur had materialized as the communicator or spokesperson for the group.

It is with love, dignity, and grace that we come to you at this time, for we are watching you—you of planet Earth. We watch as you go through your trials and tribulations. We watch as you evolve. Some of you have heard our calls. Many are awakening, and this pleases us. There are more of my kind, gathering to watch and observe as your humanity begins its ascension process. The energies are right; the time is right.

Open your hearts to hear the messages we bestow upon you.

After the meditation, I googled "Pleiades" and discovered that Steven J. Gibson, an astronomer at Arecibo Observatory in Puerto Rico, had reported that the Pleiades is also known as the Seven

Sisters.[10] (There was that number seven again!) Unlike many constellations that can be seen only in specific locations during certain times of the year, Seven Sisters is visible from almost every place on Earth, from the North Pole to south of the tip of South America, making this star cluster a perfect candidate to watch over us. The Seven Sisters is also the most obvious star cluster we can see with our unaided eyes in the night sky, so the watching goes both ways.

I entered "Zahur" in a search engine and found the word's origins. It is an Arabic name that is translated as "radiant" and "brilliant."[11] On another site, I found the Swahili translation: "flower."[12] Flower! The thoughts of this shining flower from the Pleiades propelled me back to August 28, 2013, the day I had received the first message. I realized I had come full circle. My contact with Zahur was a result of this long process of energy flow that had begun with the initial message about a flower. By keeping an open line of communication, by withholding judgment and allowing the messages to flow into my awareness, I had become a flow-er of energy.

Zahur's communication comforted me. We are not alone in the universe; there are numerous emissaries from the stars who observe us as we evolve. They not only watch us, but they also assist in our ascension process.

Each message I received paved the way for more, and each transmission provided another puzzle piece in my extraordinary adventure into the unknown. As of now, I could not tell where my adventure might lead, but perhaps one day I would know.

---

[10] naic.edu/~gibson/pleiades
[11] quranicnames.com/zahur/
[12] earthsky.org/astronomy-essentials/visible-planets-tonight

CHAPTER 6: HEAVENLY HELP

The raging storm had knocked out the electricity. "Maybe the darkness will help me hide," I thought as I cowered in the corner of my closet and tried to silence my rapid breathing. This vivid and terrifying nightmare continued as my thoughts begged over and over, "Please don't let him find me." I should have grabbed my cell phone from the bedside table when I heard him break in. I was terrified. How did he get in? The power outage must have deactivated the alarm. Nothing good could come from this, and I did not see any way to escape. I feared for my life. I felt desperate, powerless. There were evil forces set against me, and the only thing I could do was pray.

This hellish nightmare had its genesis three days earlier, on March 25, 2014, with the most innocent circumstance. I had attended a midnight meditation. The weather had turned cold, which was probably the reason why only four came to this outdoor ceremony. While meditating, I felt uncomfortable; something did not seem right. I opened my eyes and was surprised to see that the man next to me was staring in my direction and smiling. I closed my eyes and returned to the meditation. What did he want? Why the stare? Why the smile? It unnerved me.

The next day he called and emailed me several times, so any doubts I might have had about his intentions were gone. When I informed him that I had no interest in any further communications, it seemed to enrage him, and his attempts to contact me escalated. I blocked his phone calls and emails, but that didn't deter him.

When conventional methods failed to reach me, he used a different and even more terrifying tactic: he contacted me psychically. I sensed his presence when I was alone. I felt him near me when I was at work. I would turn around expecting to see him, but no one would be there. He invaded my dreams.

I did not record the details of the nightmare in my dream journal; I did not want to think about it, much less document it. I simply summarized it as "disturbing," and I ended the entry with this sentence: "I have to set up protections to keep him out of my dream space."

Set up protections? On one level I knew I needed to do that, but how? I felt overwhelmed, and I didn't know how to proceed. These feelings of helplessness brought me back to the nightmare, cowering in the corner of my closet, terrified as I hid from this predator, and prayed for help.

My journey to the unknown had changed me. With each message, I grew more sensitive as I learned to use my nonphysical senses to help expand my awareness. I had become more empathetic and understanding. My increased sensitivity to the surrounding subtle energies allowed me to experience the extraordinary while still living in an ordinary world, but this sensitivity had its downside. I had become vulnerable to negative energy.

I had learned from previous messengers about energy associated with emotions. Negative energy accompanied emotions such as jealousy, envy, or anger. When these emotions were directed at others, negative energy was sent in that direction, and this occurred whether it was intentional or not. Any negative or low energy directed at others could have debilitating results, and the more sensitive the recipient, the more profound the effects. These attacks have the potential to change a person on physical as well as emotional levels.

A number of websites[13] list common signs and symptoms of negative energy attacks, including feeling fatigued for no discernable reason, having weakness or stabbing pains in specific areas (such as the chest or upper back), and emotional reactions such as depression, sleep disturbances, irritability, anxiety, and, as I had learned through personal experience, nightmares.

I had heard of psychic attacks, but I never expected to experience them. In response to my plea, help arrived at the end of March. As I began to dictate the message, I realized my voice sounded different: it was soft and gentle. A change in voice quality was often an indicator that a new messenger had arrived.

March 29, 2014

We were watching in observance while this one participated in the meditation ceremony. It is always with protection and love that we surround her, as we did during this time.

Her thoughts are correct; the meditation was hijacked by the interfering energies of the one known as [name deleted]. [Name deleted] went beyond ethical considerations and attempted to interfere with this one's experience. We were there as a protective shield. During the meditation, this one perceived an energy field wrapped around her. This was a shield we put in place. We layered our protective energies around her.

This was true; I had felt a force field that surrounded me during the meditation. In my mind's eye, I had seen a webbed matrix wrapped around my body that insulated me like a warm blanket.

From her left side, she saw negative energies approaching. This is the side where he was. Our protection prevented the negative energies from manifesting. Those negative energies were brought on by the malcontent of this man. Because of the energy field we had set forth, he did not cause harm to this, our beloved one. We continued to maintain

---

[13] thoughtco.com/what-is-a-psychic-attack-1730541

a shield from him as he persisted in his attempts to gain this one's attention.

Another event of this sort, without his interfering energy, will result in very different outcomes, for this one will be able to soar and make further connections. This one is wise in continuing to protect her space during the dream state. We, too, will add protections for her.

I love outdoor midnight meditations, surrounded by the stillness of the evening, the sounds of nature, and only stars and the moon for lighting. I am disconnected from all electronics: no ringing phones, chiming texts, or televisions blaring. It is easy to forget about the day's worries and focus on connecting to nature and the universe.

This time, however, I did not experience any connections; I felt disappointed because nothing happened. With the exception of the mental image of the webbed matrix that covered me, nothing out of the ordinary occurred. There were no contemplative insights; in fact, the only thoughts I had were of the cold temperatures and my desire to go home.

Learning about the *"protective shield"* from the messenger changed my perspective. Although the matrix protected me from this man's negative energies, it also prevented me from experiencing any positive benefits. Suddenly, it all made sense. No wonder nothing happened.

I had pondered how to shield myself from this man during my dream state, and this message provided the answers. Just as the image of a cage of energy had protected me during the ceremony, I could do the same for myself during my dreams, but first I needed to review a couple of older messages.

Previous communications had disclosed that energy follows thought, and action follows energy. So, if I imagined a barrier around myself, I would be engaging the energy of protection. I could do this, but I felt comforted to know I would have assistance. The message continued:

There have been past lives with the one named [name deleted]. *At one time, he had been a very powerful sorcerer. He used his powers for good as well as darkness. Deep within his heart, he continues his search for power which he is seeking from this one, our beloved. She now has the tools to return to earlier lifetimes with* [name deleted]. *As she does this, she can block the energies and alter the previous patterns established with* [name deleted] *in different lifetimes that are now affecting her.*

This communication required me to review another set of messages about Points of Existence and expanded consciousness. As a person's awareness increases, more waves of the timeline are incorporated within the stretched PoE. There is direct correlation between the number of sine waves enclosed within the PoE and the likelihood of the person experiencing distortions in normally experienced time. This is the point when both future and past lives can be accessed.

I had never given much thought to past lives, so these instructions to enter the space of expanded awareness to change events through past lives left me feeling confused. Could I do this? I didn't know if I could, but I wanted to stop these negative energy attacks.

I had collected various tools to help me on my journey to the unknown. I had learned several methods to stretch my PoE in order to enter a state of expanded awareness. In addition to the more conventional methods such as meditation, prayer, and deep breathing, I had learned about using my Emotional Guidance System to increase the energy frequency surrounding my body. Having a "lighter" energy field made expanded awareness an easier state to achieve. I had also learned how to reduce brain chatter by visualization, using the formula that energy follows thought, and action follows energy.

Whether or not I endorsed the concept of past lives didn't matter. I would enter a state of expanded awareness. From there I would connect to this man's energy and set an intention to alter any previous vibrational patterns to make changes in this current time. Theoretically this sounded straightforward; I hoped I could do it.

Until then, I would ignore any skepticism I might have about past lives, and I would just proceed on my journey. No sense dwelling on ideology; I had to take care of this—the sooner, the better.

The lessons she learned during the meditation did not appear significant to her, but we gave her the tools she needed to deal with the situation with the one named [name deleted]. We helped guide her to the tools she needed to thwart the energies of [name deleted]. This one's situation that needed healing involved current, past, and future protection from the one named [name deleted]. She now has the ability to protect herself.

Lessons learned? This proved to be true. Initially I had walked away from the meditation more than a little disappointed. Although I did not understand it at the time, the sage words of the messenger made me realize how valuable the meditative experience had actually been. Not only had I been protected during the ceremony, but also enlightened. The manner in which the messengers shielded me became another tool for future use. It also opened the door to connect with what I now believe are divine, heavenly energies.

As she continues her path, we will become more open to her. There will be a brief cessation of awareness of dreams and messages due to the continual vigilance from us as we shield her from the energies of [name deleted]. When we recognize his energies are no longer a threat, there will be an allowance of further energies and information which she seeks.

She is to rest and know she is loved beyond measure, and she is protected. This protection results in a blocking of messages at the current time. She is now aware of this, and she will welcome the time when she is totally protected, and then the messages will flow again.

I felt reassured to learn of the protections put in place during the initial psychic attack. Adding protections during meditations and dreams would temporarily halt the messages. Nevertheless, I would do anything to stop these attacks.

What had begun as a desperate plea for help resulted in contact with these divine beings from the angelic realm. Once opened, this door allowed for further communication.

I heard from them again four days later. It was on a Wednesday, the first week following spring break. Although I am usually awake and out of bed a few minutes before the alarm rings, I was still operating on "spring break time," and the alarm shattered my deep sleep. I jumped out of bed and immediately took a shower to help me stay awake. While in the shower, I began to receive a message. I toweled off and grabbed my phone to record the message.

As I began my dictation, I noticed a change in my voice, and I felt calm and at total peace—quite different than what I had felt just moments before. I now associate this sense of tranquility with messengers from the angelic realm.

April 2, 2014

There are protections in place for this one. She is aware of other energies with her during the meditation ceremony. These are the energies of protection and guidance that have been with her throughout her lifetime. With this comes love and deep appreciation for the learning that has taken place in this lifetime. We have been vigilant in our protections of this one, just waiting for her awareness of us.

This energy is one of gratitude and grace as well as love. Now that the door to this energy field has opened, this one will be able to tap into this field when it is needed. It is as if her heart has discovered an additional chamber, allowing more to flood into her awareness.

We have always been with her and will remain so. This one thinks the energy is one of angelic proportion. Those are concepts humans have used to describe our energies. It is a good analogy to describe our energy fields and vibratory signatures.

As I dictated the message, I had an overwhelming feeling of being surrounded by a host of holy beings, from whom emanated grace, serenity, and peace. I felt encompassed by pure love.

The key is to ask. We have always been here but have been awaiting your request for assistance.

It felt empowering to know this energy had always been available, awaiting my request. I could sense the connection, as if a stream of energy had begun to flow to me from the angelic realm. I first saw my body fill with beautiful, soft, pink energy. It felt like I had walked into a bank of pink fog, and a sense of euphoria washed over me.

I knew my request had started a chain of energy events to make the connection possible. Help is always there; all I need to do is ask. In a download of information, the angels told me I had become a beacon, and this new energy would attract a different set of people to me. This guiding light would draw in those who needed the energy of peace and calm into their lives. The angels instructed me to wait and observe responses from other people, and so I did.

I was vigilant for the next several days, and the results were remarkable. I am all business at work, and I rarely take time for idle chat, so it is unusual for people to come by to say hello. However, over the next few days, my office seemed like it had a revolving door. In three days, I had more social visits than I'd had the previous three months combined. Even more interesting, most of these people had never been to my office before.

For example, Juliet, a physical therapist who had begun working at this elementary school eight months before, stopped by my office. I was sitting at my computer, working on a psychological report, when I heard a light tapping at my open door. I looked up and welcomed Juliet in. As she greeted me with her lovely British accent, she walked to my chair and leaned down to give me a quick kiss on the top of my head. It was a kind gesture, but certainly unusual, especially for her first visit to my office.

The next day I drove to the school district's administrative center for a meeting. As I got out of my car, I saw the principal of a school where I had previously worked. During my tenure at that school, our exchanges had never been personal. Today, however, she walked across the parking lot and greeted me with a big hug and friendly conversation. I smiled, not only at her reaction, but also at the validation it brought from the angels. As instructed, I had waited and observed. The angels were right; a different set of people had been drawn to my energy. I was becoming a believer.

I received more messages from the angelic realm about six weeks later. The following message brought me back in time to 1966.

May 13, 2014

We are a set of energies here to guide and protect you. Our doors have been open to you for many years, such as the time you almost stepped on a snake and we pulled you away from danger. This happened over fifty Earth years ago, and we now remind you of this event. You have told many people of this story.

A vision transported me back in time to my adolescent years. I walked barefooted through a field of tall grass, searching the 400-acre farm for my horse. With my horse's bridle slung over my left shoulder, I felt the cool grass beneath my bare feet. The warm sun beat down on my back in contrast to a gentle breeze that cooled my head and neck. I felt my ponytail swinging as I walked the fields.

From the perspective of both observer and participant, the speed of this internal video changed to slow motion. I walked with my head held high, and as I peered into the distance to locate my horse, something made me look down. My bare foot was inches from a large, multicolored, coiled snake.

Then it happened. It felt as if an invisible set of hands grabbed my shoulders, lifted me into the air, and pulled me away from the danger. Even now, my heart races as I think about the coiled snake within inches of my bare foot.

I remembered telling family and friends about this event. As I was stepping down, something had made me look at the ground. What had it been? When I flew up in the air, away from the snake, I had theorized it was my guardian angel who had protected me.

Now, more than fifty years later, the messenger confirmed my
theory.

*We represent a series of protective energies that have come into your
consciousness, just as other energy systems have. This is due to your
continued state of expanded awareness.*

*Although some humans perceive us as hovering above, most
humans are unaware of us. Mother Earth is transitioning, and over the
past twenty or more years, the awareness of our existence has
increased. The popularity of angels is because many from our realm are
now being perceived by humans. We have not reached into their
conscious awareness; it is just the opposite. The awareness of many
humans, partially due to Mother Earth's transition, has expanded and
has broached into our dimension.*

*Much like the attraction of a bright, sparkling light, our energies
are beacons for some humans. Some can perceive the subtle energy
frequencies of our realm and are thus attracted to us.*

*We are happy this one is aware of her ability to call upon various
energy sources such as ours. We will demonstrate to her our existence
today. We know that she does not need this proof, but we do this from
the energy of love. Today we shall be with her in an obvious, apparent
manner. Her day will be filled with small examples that are influenced
by our energies.*

This message seemed similar to the previous month's
demonstration of how others would be drawn to me as a beacon of
light, and I felt eager to see what would happen this time. As soon
as I dictated the last paragraph into my voice recorder, I found
myself taking a deep, cleansing breath that seemed to settle
throughout my entire body, filling me with a sense of peace and
happiness. I realized this intake of breath allowed the energies from
the angels' realm to enter. I began to smile as I beamed with this
new energy.

Throughout the day I experienced more acts of kindness and
compassion from others than I had for months. Although there were
no events of monumental importance, the day filled with multiple

examples of the angels' presence. Strangers met me with smiles and some with conversations. Drivers were thoughtful and considerate. The cashier at the grocery store started talking with me about the importance of gratitude. If only every day could be like this!

Later that evening as I was putting on my pajamas and getting my work clothes out for the next day, I felt a mental nudge. I stopped and took a deep breath. From seemingly out of nowhere, I realized it was only two days until my late husband's birthday. A memory from September 2, 1987, the day Daryl died, came flooding into my awareness:

While in the hospital's ICU waiting room, I had overheard a man telling his friend he had seen an angel several years before. An angel had appeared next to him on a busy street corner in Cincinnati, Ohio. It then flew in front of him and into the sky. He chuckled as he told his friend that the angel had wings on his feet.

I left the waiting room a few minutes later to return to Daryl's bedside. When the hospital's chaplain entered the room, I asked for prayers to help release my husband from his pain. Daryl was in a coma, and I knew he was ready to leave.

I took the chaplain's proffered hand, and we each placed a hand on Daryl. As I closed my eyes, I felt a deep sense of peace as I listened to the chaplain's heartfelt prayer. Then I heard him call for the "angels with winged feet" to carry Daryl home. I had never heard of angels with winged feet, but twice within the same hour made me a believer, and I knew the angels with winged feet would carry Daryl to his heavenly home. A short time later, Daryl took his last breath.

When I shared this story with my sister Eleanore, she told me the men in the waiting room were the angels in human form. She reminded me of the Bible verse in Hebrews 13:2: "Be not forgetful to entertain strangers; for thereby, some have entertained angels unaware."

The following message came as I reminisced:

Yes, we were there, and we were able to manifest in full physical form as humans, a form you could not only see but hear, for you needed to hear the words that were shared. Our full manifestations were needed, an ever-present reminder that life continues when the Earth form drops away. We manifested in physical forms in order to escort your beloved to our realm. Your ability to see us, hear us, and remember us was partially due to the close connection you had and continue to have with your husband, even when the physical body is gone. Nothing changes. The true essence continues to live on.

The angels were there in human form, waiting to escort Daryl to his heavenly home. Even more important, they verified the truth that love transcends the physical: true essence continues and does not die. The angels had fulfilled their promise of making their earlier presence known to me today, by sharing both a fifty-year-old incident, when I had been a teenager, and their presence with me, when Daryl had died twenty-seven years ago.

I had a vivid dream of angels about a year later, in May 2015. The setting in the dream was a Victorian-style house. I was in a bedroom, dressed in a long, white, flowing cotton nightgown, and I was floating about two or three feet off the ground.

Several angels floated in slow circles around me while I was suspended in midair; they blew their breath on me like whispers in the wind. I looked down and saw a tube of medicine on a bedside table. I recognized it as medicinal salve by its metallic silver cover, black screw cap, and label. One word was printed on the label: *Seraphim.* This was a healing balm created by seraphim angels.

When I woke the next morning, I found myself singing the chorus of an old spiritual song: "All night, all day, angels watching over me, my Lord. All night, all day, angels watching over me." Messages began pouring in; I retrieved my phone and recorded the following:

May 12, 2015

This one attuned to the energy of angels which allowed for contact during the dream state. This one felt angels gently blowing on her body. It is similar to a tender breeze that blows across a field of flowers. That breeze is the breath from Mother Earth herself. It comes from within her heart.

The breath this one experienced during her dream state came from angels. Just as with Mother Earth, the breath of angels also comes from the heart. It can be perceived through the body's senses, but the true perception, the perception of truth, comes when it is perceived by the heart. It is the heart that is the most sensitive organ in the human body. Perceiving through the heart is what allowed this one to recognize and acknowledge the presence of the angels.

Communication with angels occurs on a higher vibratory level, and thus it is more difficult to perceive. When humans enter a state of silence and stillness, their antennae become alerted to the more sensitive vibrations from angels. This is why our presence is often felt or acknowledged during prayer, meditation, or the dream state, for these are times when humans have entered into a higher vibratory level and are able to attune to our frequencies.

Although this one referred to seraphim, we say the name of the angel or type of angel is not as important to us as it is to humans. The name is the vibratory signature of the specific angel. Everything is energy. When the name is spoken, there is an energy vibration from the vocal cords. Those energy vibrations leave the human's body and are received by another human's ears. The energy waves vibrate in the human's ears. The human's brain translates those energies to sound. Thus, when an angel's name is spoken aloud, the name is the specific vibratory frequency connected with that angel.

The name of the angel is not as important as the energy frequency itself. Of course, there are other ways in which the signature energy frequencies can be registered. Not only can it be registered as sound as just described, but also through other human senses such as sight, touch, or smell. For those humans who are more sensitive, the signature may be recognized by a knowing or by using the "non-senses."

As soon as I recorded the message, I looked at the time. I could briefly search online about seraphim angels and about the spiritual meanings of *breath* before I got ready for work.

According to the Jewish Encyclopedia website, the seraphim are mentioned in the Christian Bible, the Book of Enoch, and the Torah.[14] Although I should have been accustomed to these uncanny synchronistic findings, what I read surprised me: The seraphim have wings on their feet! They have six wings: two to cover their faces, two for flying, and two that cover their feet. Were these the angels with winged feet that were at the hospital when my husband had died so many years before?

In Revelation 4:8, the six-winged seraphim angels are described as unceasingly singing the praises of the Lord God, the Almighty, day and night. The phrase "day and night" caught my attention, and its similarity to the "All night, all day" lyrics I had sung when I had awakened from the dream with the seraphim.

I continued my search and learned that the breath is mentioned in many religious and philosophical doctrines. The Christian New Testament and the Hebrew Bible, or Old Testament, have several references to breath, indicating this is how the Almighty gives life (Job 33: 4). Hindu philosophy refers to receiving "prana," or life-force energy, from the breath.[15] What mystical and sacred qualities were in the breath of angels in my dream?

I received a follow-up message to the dream about the seraphim angels a couple weeks later. Summer break was a few days away, and I could hardly wait. As I daydreamed one morning about how to spend my summer vacation, a message demanded to be heard. I picked up my phone and captured this message:

May 28, 2015

We came to this one in a dream about the breath of angels, for the energy we put forth is very subtle. It is a lighter, finer energy than a gentle breath, just as a gentle breath is lighter and finer than a whisper, and a whisper is lighter than speaking, and speaking is lighter than shouting. As this one continues to fine-tune her senses and tap

---

[14] jewishencyclopedia.com/articles/13437-seraphim
[15] hinduwebsite.com/hinduism/concepts/prana.asp

into the realm of non-senses, she will be able to discern the differences among us.

There are many types of beings within our realm—the realm humans refer to as the angelic realm. There is the energy of the Protector. Humans associate this subset of the angelic realm with the archangel called Michael. He is considered the leader or head of this realm.

There is also a subset for healing which humans associate with the archangel named Raphael. The energy of the Healers is different from the Protectors. There are multiple subsets within the angelic realm such as the Guardian subset. We also have a section for Awareness. It has a similar energy to the Protectors, but it is gentler.

Let us now speak of common features among the angelic realm. We are beings of higher vibrations than are found on the Earth plane. Our vibrational frequencies are subtler and finer. We respond to like energy such as when humans tap into our energy field. Many humans know in order to gain assistance from us, they need to ask for help.

We are always around, but we rarely interfere with the day to day "busyness" of life on the Earth plane unless we are asked to do so. It is the asking or the intent that sends forth an energy beacon from the human to our realm. The asking, in the form of intentions and prayers, is energy. These are of a higher vibrational frequency which more closely matches our vibrations. The energy vibrations reach the interface, the area that buffers our realm of existence from that of the humans. If the request is from the heart, the energy reaches us like a knock upon our door. We respond to like energy; when the request is from the heart, this energy reaches us like a small, brilliant spark of light that flashes.

When a prayer or intention is genuine, that energy stems from the heart. It is the heart energy of humans that represents the higher vibrational status needed in order for connections to be made into our dimension.

I saw myself in a large, cool, damp, cave in my mind's eye. Total blackness surrounded me; natural light could not enter this underground cavern. I saw a single match spark to life, and its light permeated the cave. My view changed, zooming backward, and the cave increased in size tenfold. I watched another match ignite, and as before, light filled the cave.

When there is darkness, the light of a single match is bright enough to be seen for miles; it is a call for attention. Our prayers or requests for help are our angelic beacons. Though small, our lights have enough luminous intensity to reach the angels' realm. The message continued:

> The angel realm is a subset of one of the new sets of rays from your sun. Review that information. Similar to a rainbow or the chakra system, the seven rays range in color, and each color has its own vibrational frequency. The angel realm vibrates at a very high frequency level.

As requested, I reviewed the previous messages about the seven rays in the sun as outlined in Chapter 5: Cosmic Contacts. According to this new correspondence, the angel realm resides within one of those new columns of light.

> Within each ray of energy, there are subsets, a microcosm of the macrocosm. Each of those rays is further divided into seven realms which correspond to different angels with specific frequency patterns that are associated with what humans refer to as skill sets or jobs. Humans frequently associate various archangels with specific colors due to the color pattern or vibration from their Source of existence.

When I searched "colors associated with archangels" online, many sites reported that not only were specific colors associated with different respective archangels, but so were gemstones. I also learned about a metaphysical system of angel colors based on seven different rays of light. (There's that number seven again!) The website reported that each color vibrates at a different electromagnetic energy frequency, and specific angels are associated with each specific frequency[16] —the same information I

---

[16] thoughtco.com/angel-colors-light-rays-of-angels-123826

had learned from the angels. By this time I expected to be accustomed to these eerie findings, but I wasn't. Even now, each time I validate information that had come to me from "nowhere," I am filled with a sense of wonder and excitement.

The energy from the angels felt unlike anything I had ever known. I experienced a sense of comfort knowing they were always with me, and I felt empowered when I learned to call on them. I no longer waited for extreme conditions; I had learned to ask them for assistance during many day-to-day activities: protection while driving, compassion while working with upset parents, strength and energy to complete a long week's work.

More than three years later, as I checked various upcoming spiritual classes in my area, one called "Angel Channeling" piqued my interest. I decided to attend. In June 2015, I drove to East Naples to Unity of Naples Church. I was glad that I had GPS, because the church is tucked back from the road in a beautifully wooded lot that surrounds a lake. As I parked my car and headed toward the building, I felt a sense of peace and serenity. It was as if this church rested on hallowed grounds.

I entered Fellowship Hall at Unity Church of Naples and took a seat, waiting for the class to begin. Information flooded into my awareness from the angel realm. I pulled out my notebook and started writing as fast as I could.

June 18, 2015

The energy of angels is subtle, much like the soft, gentle mist emanating from the water of a babbling brook or the mist surrounding raindrops falling from the sky. It is not the energy of the water, but instead that almost imperceptible energy of the mist that surrounds the water or rain. The energy from our realm, the angel realm, is subtle, and therefore requires recognition in order for a connection to be made. This recognition can be found within a prayer, an intention, meditation, or just a simple wish. We are always present, awaiting your recognition of us.

As loved ones enter this most sacred and beloved space, we begin to gather together, and we surround each beloved one with the golden light from our Maker. There is a hush, a sense of reverence that falls upon this sacred circle as we soften the edges of concerns and worries some of these loved ones have. We enter their energy fields, and we fill those gaps with loving, divine light.

A vision accompanied the words, and I saw myself at the church while also standing in a densely wooded forest. I looked up and saw thousands of miniature stars. The sky began to fall, and these golden sparkles descended on me like a gentle mist. As pastel pink and green bands of energy gently wove back and forth in this haze of golden glitter, the tiny flecks of light began to twinkle as if awakening from a deep slumber. The energy blanketed the room where the twenty-seven participants were seated in a semicircle.

Our energy helps our loved ones breathe a little easier and deeper. As our loved ones breathe in, they take in this beautiful energy we share with this beloved group.

We see the energy of the group begin to ascend toward our realm, thus beginning to raise the veil separating our dimensions. As this sacred group's energy is lifted, even more angels from our realm descend into this room. It is with total love that we welcome this energy. It is with respect and gratitude that we acknowledge each and every precious soul in attendance. Welcome, beloved ones.

The words of the message and the images of the pastel ribbons of energy floating among blinking sparkles of light brought me to tears. This powerful yet serene energy helps *"soften the edges of concerns and worries"* by entering our energy fields and filling our *"gaps with loving, divine light."* This accurately described my own feeling; it was as if the angels reached deep inside me to touch my soul.

The group's intention sent forth an energy invitation for angels to connect. As they answered our calls, vibrational entrainment occurred, and the frequency signature of the prayer, meditation, or intention became synchronized with angelic vibratory patterns. This opened the door for future contact because it raised the veil separating our dimensions. The results strengthen when the prayer or meditation occurs in a group.

The collective power of group energy magnifying prayers is not a new concept. Matthew 18:20 states, "For where two or three are gathered together in my name, there am I in the midst of them." The collective energy of the meditation group combined with the sacred grounds of Unity Church set the stage for powerful and profound spiritual experiences. We were primed and ready to receive the healing energies from the angels and the loving messages shared by Gigi Petersen, a gifted psychic who channeled the sacred words from the angels. Although I did not know any of the participants beforehand, I had become part of their family before the meditation had ended. I felt a sense of harmony and unity not only with my brothers and sisters in the group but also with others throughout the world. The presence and messages from the angels confirmed we were not separate; we were part of the sacred connection to all that is.

An angelic presence fills the heart with love and joy. Angels surround us and guard us, but they often work behind the scenes. They have been with me throughout my life, protecting me as a teen by pulling me away from a coiled snake. Wrapping their wings around me, they shielded me from people who wished to harm me. Angels have visited in dreams, spoken through messages, and manifested in full physical form as humans in a time of great need in my life.

My life has been blessed and enriched by angels. Their presence is pervasive; they are always watching and ready to heed our cries for help. Angels were here when we entered the world, and they will accompany us when it is our time to exit. Their willingness to come to our aid brings us solace even in our darkest hours, offering peace, protection, and serenity. It is a comfort to know we are never alone.

CHAPTER 7: STAMPEDE

L ife began to get interesting in the months leading up to October 2015. My daughter, Cassie, had announced she was expecting another baby girl, due to arrive May 2016. I was thrilled at the prospect of becoming a grandmother again, and I knew three-year-old Lorelai was excited to become a big sister.

My job was going well, but each school year seemed to bring more work. I wondered if there was more to do or whether it just felt that way. Regardless, by the time Friday night arrived each week, I felt exhausted, and I looked forward to the weekend so I could recuperate. When my friend Scott invited my friend Maria and me to join him for a meditation that involved Reiki and crystal bowls, I welcomed this opportunity to relax, and I hoped it would help me feel a sense of renewal.

Reiki, according to *Medical News Today,* is a form of energy healing. In "Reiki: What is it and what are the benefits?" Tim Newman reports that Reiki involves "the transfer of universal energy from the practitioner's palms to their patient."[17] As the Reiki healer places his or her hands a few inches above the client's body, it helps the energy flow to remove blockages in a manner similar to acupuncture or acupressure.

Crystal bowls heal through sound vibrations caused by suede-covered cylindrical mallets that are moved around the bowls'

---

[17] medicalnewstoday.com/articles/308772.php

outside rims. The Rhys Thomas Institute, in an article entitled "Understanding the Bowls," stated that playing crystal bowls is a "form of vibrational medicine based on the scientific principles that all matter, and most importantly the cells in your body, vibrate to a precise frequency when healthy and to a dissonant frequency when in dis-ease."[18] Using tuned, deep-vibration crystal bowls can balance these frequencies and bring them back into harmony.

Scott, Maria, and I headed to neighboring Fort Myers to attend the crystal bowl Reiki meditation at the Church of Spiritual Light, an all-faith, all-denominational church. Although I had attended both crystal bowl meditations and Reiki sessions, I had not experienced them simultaneously. I wondered how the combination of these healing modalities would feel.

When we arrived at the church, we entered a large, comfortable room. We saw nine or ten people sitting or lying on blanketed mats that surrounded a set of crystal bowls in the center of the room. The dimmed lighting and soft background music seemed to invite the participants to relax. We saw three mats together that offered a perfect niche for us to settle. This welcoming space beckoned us to slip into our places without breaking the spell of quietude and reverence that permeated the air.

After we nestled in, the Reverend Renee Bledsoe welcomed the group, and the meditation began. She positioned herself outside the circle to hold prayerful space for the event while a young woman sat on a large cushion in the center of the room and played the bowls. Reiki practitioners Linda and Al began the session. Each worked half of the circle to ensure everyone would receive healing.

Something extraordinary happened to me in the time between Reverend Bledsoe's welcome and the few seconds before the meditation began. As Reverend Bledsoe began fading the background music to welcome the vibrations from the crystal bowls, I heard it: the almost inaudible beat of a drum. The faint drumbeat called me to follow and embark on a different path. It served as a catalyst to launch me into another realm of existence.

---

[18] healingcrystalbowls.com

When I looked at Maria and Scott to get their attention, their closed eyes told me I was wasting my time. No matter how much I willed them to look at me, they remained blissfully at rest.

Messages began to flow, and in my mind, a voice said the sound of the drum represented the heartbeat of Grandfather Sky. Immediately within my mind's eye, a vortex opened at the top of the room where the meditation had just begun. The vortex was spinning like a miniature tornado. I could not believe what I saw. An interdimensional portal—a breach in the universe—had opened before my very own eyes.

The ancestors were the first to arrive. This large gathering of Native Americans entered and then congregated at the back of the room before they turned to face the portal. Their full halt seemed to offer an invitation for the next group, the wisdom keepers of the tribe, the Council of Elders. Although fewer in number, the force radiating from the Council of Elders suggested immeasurable strength, power, and knowledge. They crossed the threshold into our dimension, and like the ancestors before them, they circled the perimeter of the room in ceremonial style before they paused to face the whirling vortex. All eyes were on the center of the room when a host of angels drifted through the interdimensional doorway. Tears filled my eyes. The angels seemed to be surrounded by a cloud of pure love and compassion. They joined the gathering in the rear of the room and turned in apparent anticipation of events to come.

The groups arranged themselves in elevated rows; their tiered positions allowed unobstructed views of the center of the room. They stood motionless with their eyes on the vortex as they awaited the main event. Excitement pushed aside the solemn and reverent mood of the room like leaves in a storm.

I found myself eager with anticipation for what would happen next. Like the visitors in the back of the room, my eyes watched the portal, but unlike them, I had no idea what I was waiting for.

I watched with astonishment as a newborn buffalo calf on wobbly legs entered through the portal. It was pure white with a tinge of pink on the nose, inside the ears, and on the rim of the lids surrounding its milky blue eyes. I noticed movement at the mouth of the portal and expected to see the calf's mother arrive. Instead, a beautiful Native American woman entered and stood by the calf's side.

The two remained at center stage and floated near the mouth of the portal. The tiers of ancestors, Council of Elders, and angels had paved the way for this main event; their ceremonial procession honored the entrance of the white buffalo calf and the woman.

As this vision came to a close, I received the following message:

October 19, 2015

The white buffalo calf represents the energy manifestation of what is required for healing. It represents innocence, complete surrender, purity, passion, the open heart, and playfulness of the child. When you are in a state of innocence, a state of awe, a state of acceptance, a state of purity, anything and everything are possible. All healing takes place when this occurs. This is the energy required for miracles.

I knew about angels, but Grandfather Sky, Council of Elders, and ancestors were new to me. And what about the white buffalo calf? The vivid details and the message surprised me. Although this was new territory for me, I decided to go with the flow.

The meditation ended, and the ringing of the bowls slowed and then stopped. With the lights still dimmed, most participants sat up and turned toward the center of the room, but I continued to scribble my experiences in my notebook. When I glanced around and noticed my out-of-sync position with the others, I stopped writing and turned to face the center of the room.

From outside the circle where she had been holding space for the event, Reverend Bledsoe asked if anybody wished to speak. As a first-time visitor to the church, I felt hesitant, yet I wanted to share these vivid and puzzling experiences. I raised my hand and described what I had seen. When I had finished speaking, Reverend Bledsoe asked me a series of questions:

1. Did I know the church was founded on the philosophy of the medicine wheel?

No, I did not. I did not even know what that meant; I only knew "medicine wheel" referred to something in Native American culture.

2. Did I know the church had a John of God Crystal Healing Bed?

No, I did not. Reverend Bledsoe told me the church houses a lighted crystal bed from a Brazilian healer named John of God. (Little did Reverend Bledsoe know that I actually owned one of these.) The bed operates as a portal through which the entities who work with this Brazilian healer can enter to assist with healing. I had envisioned a portal open at the top of the room. Could this be the portal from the John of God Crystal Healing Bed?

3. Did I know a picture of White Buffalo Calf Woman hung on the wall adjacent to the John of God Crystal Healing Bed?

No, I did not. Who? She must have been the Native American woman I saw with the white buffalo calf. And although a painting of White Buffalo Calf Woman should have been an obvious clue, months passed before I realized she was an important legend in Native American culture.

4. Did I know about the other painting in the room with the John of God Crystal Healing Bed that depicted a portal surrounded by tiers of ancestors, angels, and the Council of Elders?

No, I did not. Who were the Council of Elders and the ancestors? Reverend Bledsoe said Al, one of the Reiki healers in the meditation, had painted this picture, and it hung on the wall at the foot of the John of God Crystal Healing Bed.

I felt bewildered at the eerie and uncanny connections. The faint drumbeat had summoned me to enter some sort of other-dimensional space and allowed me to witness these strange visions. I had seen tiers of ancestors, the Council of Elders, and angels, and they had entered the room through a portal. I felt like I had stepped inside Al's painting—a portal surrounded by tiers of the ancestors, the Council of Elders, and angels. How could that be?

A white buffalo calf and a Native American woman entered through the portal with a message about miracles and healing. In the next room, a painting of White Buffalo Calf Woman hung on a wall adjacent to a portal—the John of God Crystal Healing Bed. How did I know these things? I shook my head in disbelief.

And so began my relationship with the spirit of White Buffalo. Even more astonishing events would occur soon: I heard directly from White Buffalo a few days after my first visit to the Church of Spiritual Light.

October 31, 2015

I am the spirit of White Buffalo. I sit upon a seat in the Council of Elders. I come to you through the spirit of those who have come before. I come through the Council of Elders and through the spirit of ancestors. I come to you. I enter upon this sacred ground that has been set forth with the intention of being a portal between worlds. I have been called forth, and now I enter to hear thy call. I came forth to this one as a calf, a small white buffalo calf. The calf is one of innocence and purity. It represents the true essence of my spirit.

As I dictated the message into my voice recorder, within my mind I saw a picture of White Buffalo Calf Woman. Long hair flowed down her back, and although I could not estimate her age, I sensed her youth and wisdom. She wore white buffalo skins fashioned as a dress.

As I viewed the picture of her in my mind's eye, I looked to see if she wore moccasins, but I could not see her feet. The following message came in response to my curiosity about her footwear:

She walks upon this Earth with bare feet so she can feel the energy of Mother Earth.

Round and oblong turquoise beads adorned the fringes on the sleeves and the hem of her dress. As I marveled at the beauty of the turquoise beads, unspoken words said the blue represented the color of the eyes of White Buffalo. I recalled the milky blue eyes of the newborn white buffalo calf I had seen at my first visit to the Church of Spiritual Light. The message continued:

I clothe myself with the skin of White Buffalo, and I call with a buffalo drum made from the skin of White Buffalo. White Buffalo is of purity, strength, wisdom, and power. White Buffalo sits high upon the Council of Elders and is called to enter the dimension of Mother Earth at this time.

I, White Buffalo Calf Woman, represent White Buffalo. I am here to call forth those who are willing to listen, those who are willing to hear my drum as they feel this beat within their hearts. I enter this dimension through White Buffalo Calf, calling to those who are able to hear and see. I call to those who are able to answer the call of the white buffalo drum as it beats to the sacred rhythm from the Council of Elders. I call to those who are attuned to our energy, our field of existence.

White Buffalo Calf Woman representing White Buffalo? This would suggest a third entity: White Buffalo, White Buffalo Calf Woman, and White Buffalo Calf.

It is time for all to come together in peace. It is time for all humans upon Mother Earth to embrace the oneness of all, to recognize their divinity and source of spirit.

As ceremonies occur in this most sacred place [referring to the Church of Spiritual Light], *my spirit will be felt, for I am with you. White Buffalo Calf is the conduit for healing that enters upon the sound of the buffalo drum. White Buffalo Calf brings the energy of the healing from the Medicine Wheel of the Elders. White Buffalo Calf Woman brings the connection from the heart of the Medicine Wheel to you. Both come to you as a bridge to connect our dimensions. Be ye one of spirit with us. Let us send peace, love, and healing to Mother Earth and all of her inhabitants. Awaken to us and to your true nature. Let there be peace and healing on Mother Earth.*

I felt the power behind the messages as I spoke these words into my recorder. This commanding trinity of White Buffalo, White Buffalo Calf, and White Buffalo Calf Woman shared their compelling messages of interdimensional connections and the awakening for peace and healing on Earth.

These words astonished me on multiple levels, but I maintained my mantra to stay open. I did not want to shut any doors; I wanted more information. By withholding judgment and allowing the information to flow, my journey gained incredible momentum.

Almost a month had passed, and it was a Sunday night. For the first time, the school district where I worked had incorporated Thanksgiving with a fall break. I was so excited about having the upcoming week off that I had difficulty falling asleep. When I finally dozed off, White Buffalo visited me.

In the middle of a dream of haphazard scenarios that made no sense, time seemed to stand still, and all the swirling images faded. I felt a presence, and I turned to see who it was. Standing tall within a deeply forested background, I saw a Native American male who was looking in my direction; I knew this was White Buffalo. He wore some sort of beaded breastplate made from bone, beads, and leather on his bare chest. I could feel the strength and power from him as his thoughts conveyed to me that he had a message he wished to share. This must have been the spiritual equivalent to a text chime!

As soon as I awoke the next morning, I went to my computer to document the words ready to come forth. White Buffalo gave me basic laws or tenets to live by; he told me that White Buffalo Calf represented the new Earth, the spirit of new Gaia.

November 22, 2015

I come to you in peace. New times have arrived. This is a new Earth, a new Earth upon which you shall live—a new day, a new world, a new Earth.

Tenet #1: Honor

Religious texts say to honor thy mother and father. This is a basic tenet calling for you to honor thy Source. We say to honor thy Mother

127

Earth/Gaia and Father/Grandfather Sky. Honor all living things, not only those that breathe. Honor all that surround you, for you are a part of this. You are not separate. This is you. Use the senses that were given to you by Source. Use those senses to experience the world differently. When you engage the energy of honor, your senses open. Your experiences and interactions become richer.

Tenet #2: Respect

Respect your neighbors. Your neighbors are not only those who live amongst you or within your clan but those who live within your tribe as well. Respect your enemies. Respect the strangers who walk upon this Earth. Respect not just humans, but plants, minerals, and animals. Share with them, honor and respect them, for they are part of all, as are you.

Tenet #3: Love

Love. Love is what motivates humans. Love is what challenges humans. Love makes us look at things in a different light. Love allows us to see another person's point of view. Love is all-encompassing. Love is what brings us together as a clan, as a tribe. Love is glue that binds hearts together. Love is.

Tenet #4: Obey Your Heart

This is the greatest law of all. Obey your heart. As you obey your heart, everything else will fall in alignment with the greater good. Learn this lesson from our animal friends. Watch how they go about their lives. They live not in the spaces of their brains, but they flow in a natural way by living moment to moment. They follow their hearts, for the heart will never lead you astray. Your path, guided by your heart, will be the path of perfect alignment. So be it.

Tenet #5: Forgiveness

Forgive and ask forgiveness. The act of forgiveness opens deeply embedded wounds of the warrior. The act of forgiveness is a powerful salve of the Great Medicine Man. Opening the wound takes a concerted effort, and it is not without pain, yet opening the wound is necessary for healing to occur. The energy of forgiveness is a salve to cool the intense, fiery pain that has been inflicted. Forgiveness allows all healing to take place. When forgiveness is withheld, the wound continues to fester. It stays inflamed, and infection spreads. Old wounds may be buried deep within. Unless they have been treated with the salve of forgiveness, they will never heal.

When a poisoned dart is removed from flesh, its poison continues to infect surrounding tissue. The poison enters the bloodstream. Unless the wound itself is healed, damage continues. Cells, organs, and vital strength are affected. There must be healing, complete healing. This healing, my friend, is for everyone, not only the injured. With the salve of forgiveness, the injured is restored to a state of good health. Forgiveness also removes the energy of karma. We are all one. Forgiveness is needed to bring everyone back into the state of wholeness and oneness. The energy of forgiveness brings forth alignment with Source.

These tenets represent a new way spirit is moving through this one; it is part of the new Gaia. Spirit speaks to us in different ways. Some through ancestors, some through feeling, some through music, some through art, some through dance, some through knowing. Some messages are too subtle to perceive, yet there is a gentle nudge, a hint, a suggestion. We operate a little differently than before but with no discernable reason why. We do not perceive the guidance, yet we allow Guidance to lead us down a different path.

Spirit of White Buffalo is coming to this new Gaia in the form of White Buffalo Calf. There are similarities between White Buffalo Calf and other ascended masters. Jesus Christ came to Earth as did White Buffalo Calf. Both come from spirit, from Source. White Buffalo Calf is a part of the Source of all there is. This Source is referred to as White Buffalo. Jesus Christ came from spirit, from Source. He is from the Source of all there is. This Source is referred to as God, Holy Father, Creator. This analogy is the same for all the ascended masters that have come upon this Earth. We say it is true for each of you as well.

Each human upon this Earth has come from Source, from the energy of all that is. As with White Buffalo Calf, Jesus Christ, and all ascended masters, they carry aspects of Source with them upon this Earth plane. They are representations of Source, as you are. Each of you is a part of the whole; you are the whole. There are many names that have been given: Star Seed, Divine Spark, Dream Seed, etc., but we say these are only words. Humans stem from Source regardless of the name given to the Source. With the new Gaia, the time has come for each human to return to Source, to awaken to the truth within that we are all one.

White Buffalo Calf came to this one as a newborn calf, for this represents newness and birth; it is a manifestation of new beginnings. It is time to look at these old messages with a new light, these messages that have been received for millennia.

There have been messages shared with those on the Earth plane, but these messages have been distorted. Not all distortions have been intentional, but messages were interpreted literally. When messages result in exclusivity and not inclusivity, know there has been misinterpretation.

We are all one. We repeat, we are all one. There is not "us versus them." We look upon the centuries of so-called holy wars upon the Earth and know there is ignorance, a miscommunication of our messages. How can any religion claim ownership to Source? How can there be only one path to Source? How can both sides fight in the name of Source and each side claim their side to be true? God Source represents all. God Source is all. We are all one. We are all one. Our messages are of inclusivity, not exclusivity. Do you love your right eye more than your left?

Tenet #6: Harmony

Harmony is like the strong undercurrent in a river. It is always there, and it is very powerful. Although not always visible on the surface, the undercurrent guides and directs the flow of the river. Harmony is an undercurrent in life. It is in this current of harmony that everything flows from Source. Harmony is the foundation of all there is. It is the glue that holds everything together. It is a natural phenomenon that will bind all things so they will operate in fullness, wholeness, and unity.

When you look to Father Sky at night, you may see only a sliver of the moon. Yet the fullness of Grandmother Moon is always there but not always seen. Harmony is like the moon: always there in its fullness but not always perceived.

It is time for humans to let go of preconceived notions of what is important. It is time to live life through the heart center. By living in *fullness and through the heart, one engages the energy of harmony. The heart center beckons, and the energy of harmony answers. Harmony will begin to flow as rapidly as a river filled with the melting snow of winter. It is the natural way. It is our way. It is time for humanity to return to the way of nature, the way of spirit, the way of the White Buffalo.*

The tenets came fast, and I typed as quickly as possible to capture each word of this rapid download. I felt almost overwhelmed by the messages and the underlying universal truth that we are all one. I needed time to process this profound message. It is with great hope that these tenets would help return humankind to *"the path of Oneness, the path of Love, the path of Truthfulness."*

A couple weeks later, Maria and I attended a meditation at a small center only a couple of blocks from her house. As we were welcomed into the center, we noticed that there were only five participants. The leader guided us through a peaceful meditation in which we were to imagine meeting with our guides or angels. During this process, I received messages for each participant from several sources, but White Buffalo spoke to only one person. He came to me with a specific message for Maria.

December 3, 2015

It is the beat of the drum that is your calling. Listen, Dear One, to the beat of the drum, for it is your guidepost. The beat of the drum is sacred for it represents the energy of the heart. It is not only the heart of your human body, but the energy of the heart of Mother Earth. You are connected to all that is. You are all that is. Within you lies wisdom beyond measure. Tap into that wisdom by following the beat of the drum. We have been with you for many lifetimes, and we are pleased you are beginning to acknowledge our connections.

We say to you to throw off the breastplate you have built for protection.

In my mind's eye, I saw a detailed picture of a Native American warrior's breastplate made from animal bones and beads that were held together by leather straps. The picture morphed into another breastplate, one with ancient Egyptian ancestry.

The spirit of White Buffalo has indigenous origins and neither time nor location could bind it. It emanates the energy of ascension and it represents Egyptians as well as spirits beyond the Earth. The message continued:

I say to you, throw off your breastplate, for its original purpose is spent. It no longer serves you as protection; it now holds you as its captive. It holds you back from the recognition of your truth. Allow the energy frequency of the drumbeat to permeate your breastplate. Allow the energy frequency of the drumbeat to shatter the bones that now serve as your prison cell, holding your true nature captive. It is time, my Dear Sister, to toss off your armor, and throw it upon the grasses of this Earth. Allow it to follow its own course and return to its origin. Let go of the burden of the breastplate. It is heavy, weighing you down. Honor its purpose as you release it back into Mother Earth. It has served you well but is now holding you back.

As you honor and release the walls of your imprisonment back into the energy of Mother Earth, become as the newborn child. Breathe in. Breathe in the breath of life just as a newborn takes a first breath. There is newness; a new life awaits you. Be not fearful for the beat of the drum will be your guide. The beat of the drum will be heard by your heart. Your heart will align itself with the beat of this drum, the drum of White Buffalo spirit feeling the beat of Mother Earth and all her inhabitants. Once free from captivity, your heart will sing. Let it sing to the beat of my drum.

A personal communication had replaced the universal messages I usually receive from White Buffalo. When I shared this with Maria, she said it made her feel part of something bigger, as if she carried knowledge of lessons learned over many lifetimes.

The message about the breastplate protecting her from pain rang true. She admitted hiding her authentic self behind her closed heart. Maria understood the wisdom of White Buffalo's words telling her to release her fears. By freeing her heart from its imprisonment, she would allow good things to come into her life. It was time for change.

In March 2016, Maria, Scott, and I returned to Fort Myers to visit the Church of Spiritual Light for another crystal bowl Reiki event. Over the months, we had become regulars at these meditations, and although it was an hour drive, the warm welcome from Reverend Bledsoe and the Reiki practitioners, Linda and Al, made the trip worthwhile. We always felt renewed and energized after the meditations. The Church of Spiritual Light was beginning to feel like my home away from home. Not surprisingly, as the meditation began this night, White Buffalo arrived first on the scene.

"Healing—you receive what you need."

These words from White Buffalo arrived before the meditation had begun. He said he prepared each participant to receive the full bounty of the healing frequencies offered.

While relaxing in the meditation, I began to visualize colors. I saw several colorful ribbons of energy, and I knew they represented the tiers of spirits from my first visit: ancestors, Council of Elders, and angels. The brightly colored ribbons wafted above the participants' heads and danced in slow motion before mingling together to create new colors—a mystical dance of creation.

The patterns and colors mesmerized me. I realized these sacred and holy energy ribbons represented the vibrations of wisdom and healing from White Buffalo as well as from the crystal bowls, Reiki, and the John of God Crystal Healing Bed. Once I realized these sacred connections, as if on cue, the message continued:

We have risen. We are not a separate path to Source, for we recognize there are multiple paths to the top of the mountain. Our paths intertwine and meet as we navigate toward Source. There are many paths to traverse. Over time these moccasins have crossed the tracks of other tribes, religions, and cultures. All the paths are now combining to give us more direction to our higher selves.

So together, Dear One, we traverse the paths to home, the paths we have longed for, leading us to truth, love, justice, and harmony. We walk upon these trails with our heads held high and our hearts open wide. We open to accept the divine healing energies from Source.

When I heard those words, I felt overcome with emotion, and tears ran down my face. Although my heart knew I wanted to follow a true and authentic spiritual path, I had fallen short of this goal. Like a feather adrift in a spring breeze, I found myself relinquishing all resistance as I whispered to myself, "I surrender. I surrender. I surrender with love."

As I listened to the celestial harmonies of the crystal bowls, the vision changed, and crystalline starbursts formed above each meditation participant. These bright white patterns of light resembled iridescent stars or snowflakes suspended in a dark blue night sky. White Buffalo told me these intricate patterns represented fragments of the divine spark of Source—alive, vibrant, and unique to each individual's energy field.

These cosmic patterns stretched horizontally, forming a circle of light around the room. The ring pulsated, and its light grew more intense until it burst into multiple threads of energy that exploded toward the center of the room before they combined into a single powerful vertical shaft of light.

When the final threads of energy entered the newly formed beam of light, it began spiraling upward before disappearing near the ceiling, as if it exited through a doorway to another dimension. Could this be the same portal from my first visit to the church? The message continued:

There is no self; there is only one.
  The one path.
  The one spark.

To knowingness.
To everything.
To you.

It is all there is. We are all one, and that is all there is. It is time to come to the realization we are all there is.

As we continue this path to truth, we constantly blend our energies with all there is.

We are led by the purity of the spirit of White Buffalo, for he is the foundation of this most holy ground. It is he who leads us into the portal, the portal to self. The only requirements are the openness of our hearts and the letting go of those energies that no longer serve us.

For there is no "you." There is only one — the all there is.

The initial message of healing and receiving what you need ended with a display of dancing ribbons of light aligned with each person's energy. I knew this light gathered specific data for healing. This energy combined into a single shaft of light designed to carry our individual prayers and intentions through an interdimensional portal where healing would manifest. I did not know the destination beyond the vortex, but I knew it held sacred energies from the ancestors, Council of Elders, angels, and White Buffalo.

How many times had prayer for physical healing resulted in something else? Healing takes place on many levels, and I knew I needed a spiritual healing. I tearfully surrendered and allowed it to occur. As I relinquished any attachments to outcomes, I knew each of us in the healing circle would receive what we needed.

As the last threads of light exited through the portal, White Buffalo's message spoke of unity. We are expressions of the whole, but we are not separate. When a wave breaks in the middle of the ocean, it's briefly suspended before falling back into the water. A drop of spray from the crest of the wave might appear as separate, but it's not; it's a small, brief expression of the whole that then returns, indistinguishable, to the fullness of the ocean.

We do the same, assuming individual identities instead of viewing our unity and totality. During our time on Earth, we represent individual expressions of the whole. *"We are all one, and*

that is all there is. It is time to come to the realization we are all there is."
If we would embrace this concept, could we eliminate fighting and
bickering among our friends and family? If we saw ourselves as
expressions of the whole and not separate, could we eliminate war?
How could prejudices exist if we knew we were all one?

These words resonated with me, but they also presented a
challenge. Would I embrace these truths, and let them help guide
my life? Would I take the necessary steps to walk a more spiritual
path? I saw this as part of my healing. I could talk the talk, but
would I walk the walk?

After several contacts with White Buffalo and White Buffalo Calf
Woman, I began to recognize when they wished to communicate.
Reminders often came through dreams, errant thoughts, and
sometimes a knowing. By the end of March and the first part of
April 2016, I had ignored many such suggestions; apparently, I
needed more direct measures to secure my attention.

During the first week of April, I was surprised by a call from
Katherine, a woman I had met at The Monroe Institute in Virginia.
Although she and I followed each other through various social
media, we had never spoken on the telephone before. Her call
surprised me.

After a brief hello, Katherine said she felt compelled to call me.
Although she did not know why, we both knew the reason for her
call would eventually be revealed. In the meantime, we talked
about family, friends, and changes in our lives since our last visit to
The Monroe Institute the previous year. Our conversation turned to
one of our favorite subjects: exploration of consciousness. What
Katherine said next surprised me.

Katherine told me she saw a vision of White Buffalo Calf
Woman moments before she called. My heartbeat quickened when I
heard those words. I had never heard of White Buffalo Calf Woman
until six months before, so Katherine's words filled me with
anticipation and excitement.

I told Katherine of my introduction to White Buffalo Calf Woman, and as I shared the story, in the back of my mind I understood the reason for her call—another not-so-subtle reminder that White Buffalo and White Buffalo Calf Woman were trying to reach me. Now I could add phone calls to White Buffalo's methods to get my attention.

A couple of weeks later, I carved out some time to receive a message. It was mid-April, and I was counting down the six weeks until summer break. On this Sunday afternoon, I was beginning to prepare for the workweek ahead. I had finished my household chores, and I had no more reasons to postpone receiving the message. I'm not sure why I procrastinated; perhaps it was just my stubborn nature appearing when I least expect it. White Buffalo had tried to reach me through stray thoughts, dreams, and even phone calls. I knew these were attempts to contact me, but I had been too busy with my day-to-day activities to comply.

After many subtle and not-so-subtle hints, it was the lyrics of a song that became the tipping point. I finally succumbed, unable to ignore the requests any more. Over and over in my mind, I sang, "Buffalo girl won't you come out tonight, come out tonight, come out tonight." It was an earworm—it would not stop! So, after what had turned out to be a two-week delay, I finally turned on my computer and opened my online journal. Immediately, the words rushed out, and my typing flooded the screen like water bursting through a dam.

April 17, 2016

It is time. It is time to awaken. I am here and will give voice to those who are ready to listen, ready to hear the words that have been passed from generation to generation, for eons upon eons. The time is right. The time is ripe. Much like a tomato on a vine that is ready to split open, there is a swelling of energy upon the Earth plane as Gaia makes her transition to the realm of spirit. She brings those of the Earth plane along with her.

Among those making this transition are others, such as this one, whose eyes have opened, whose ears have opened and most important, whose hearts have opened. These are the ones ready to receive the word from ancestors and spirits that have been guarding Gaia, protecting Gaia. We welcome you to hear our voices and to decide for yourself your chosen path, for there is a choice. Many may wish to remain blissfully ignorant. We say these are honorable paths if this is what they have chosen. Some may wish to be voices for those willing to listen. We honor these paths as well.

All paths are guided by the heart, for only the heart knows the true path of spirit. There are many paths to the top of the mountain, and each is guided by the heart. No one path is truer than the other; each is attuned to the energy frequency of the seeker's heart. Some paths lead directly to Source; others are more circuitous.

Many follow a path without knowing it is directed by the heart. The Great Awakening is taking place on Gaia. As part of the Great Awakening, the heart is recognized for its powerful and honor-bound role. It is the journey many ancestors have traveled.

Ages ago, long before humans had language, my people lived a simple and pure life. We lived as one with Mother Earth, her plants, her animals, her minerals. We communicated with star people, and we used the guidance of our hearts for all aspects of life. We learned to live off the land, growing crops, fishing, and hunting. We respected all forms of life, and we recognized the relationships we as humans had with all of nature. We would hunt animals for food, clothing, and shelter. This was done with reverence toward the animals. As humans, we recognized the role each of us played in this most reverent and honorable relationship.

As Gaia transitions to higher dimensions, we see the veil thinning, and more humans hear our call. We acknowledge and also rejoice, for our voices can be heard. With this transformation on Gaia, life will continue to change on the Earth plane. As it was when I, spirit of White Buffalo, walked the path of Earth, the heart will become the guiding force for all humans. The need for vocal communication will be less. Humans will use the heart as the organ for communication. As this occurs there will be clarity in communication—clarity that has not been witnessed on Gaia since before the development of language.

For the heart is becoming the center of the new society, returning to its proper place among all living things.

The message faded then stopped. Because Katherine's phone call had encouraged me to connect with White Buffalo, I decided to email her the message. Within a few minutes, she called, and I informed her about the earworm that had begun shortly after our initial phone call a couple of weeks before. I said those monotonous, rhythmical lyrics had become the catalyst, the final straw, for me to open myself to receive White Buffalo's message. Taking time to do so offered relief from the unrelenting chorus:

> Buffalo girl won't you come out tonight
> Come out tonight, come out tonight.
> Buffalo girl won't you come out tonight
> And we'll dance by the light of the moon.

I associated this song with winter holidays because the first time I heard it was in Frank Capra's classic movie *It's a Wonderful Life*, which plays every Christmas season. But even with my limited exposure to it, something did not seem right. I searched for the lyrics online and discovered the problem. The words playing in my mind differed; I heard Buffalo "girl," not Buffalo "gals." Although the difference puzzled me, I didn't think much about it at the time.

When I told Katherine the girl/gals wording discrepancy, she knew it referred to my unborn granddaughter. Without sharing this intuitive thought, Katherine asked whether "girl" might refer to my granddaughter. I wondered aloud whether it was three-year-old Lorelai or her soon-to-be baby sister Shalane. As I spoke Shalane's name, cold chills racked my body. Over the years, I had learned that cold chills represented validation of truths, so I knew the Buffalo "girl" in the song referenced Shalane. But why?

Katherine also felt chills. Our co-validation of Shalane as the Buffalo girl in the song triggered a chain of events that pushed the boundaries of my ever-increasing belief system even farther. Things happened that I would have never thought possible, and I am not certain I would have believed it were it not for Katherine as my witness.

An image of my daughter, Cassie, formed in my mind. She was sleeping on her back on an overstuffed featherbed. I watched as a tanned white buffalo hide floated from above to cover her pregnant belly. The following message arrived as I described this scenario to Katherine:

The White Buffalo skin is to protect this one [Shalane] *and her mother in preparation to bring her into this world.*

White Buffalo told me the tanned side of the hide that lay against my daughter protected her while the white curly hair on top attracted his energies, absorbing them like a sponge. Through the filter of this spirit blanket, the *"final energy frequencies"* from White Buffalo entered Shalane.

The spirit of the White Buffalo courses through the veins of this wee one. It is the energy of wisdom and strength. It is the energy of kindness and understanding. It is the energy of balance needed upon Gaia today. Coursing through her veins is the power of the ancestors and the power of healing not only for Gaia but for humankind.

With these words, Katherine and I felt a shift of energy as a rift opened between dimensions. Katherine saw a herd of buffalo running toward an open gate in a large fenced area. As she described her vision, the most remarkable thing happened—I saw it too! We shared the vision.

White Buffalo told me the opened gate represented a portal from spirit for his energy to enter Earth's dimension. To the right of the opened gate, a little girl dressed in cowgirl boots stood on the lowest rung of the wood fence. This little girl appeared to be around age three; she had light-colored hair, and her short, brightly colored dress flew in the wind created by the stampeding buffalo. She giggled with delight as the herd charged through the gate.

Although she was not yet born, we both understood that the little girl was Shalane.

I felt the ground shake as the thunderous hooves rushed toward the opening in the fence. I do not know how or why, but Katherine and I served as witnesses for this event. We knew Shalane would be born with the sacred energies of White Buffalo in her soul.

The impact of this profound event rendered us speechless. Instead of relying on my professional training as a psychologist to help process this intense experience, we changed the subject. Katherine asked about the preparations for the baby's arrival, including the nursery's decorations.

I had an epiphany as I told Katherine details of Shalane's bedroom. A wave of understanding washed over me as I realized White Buffalo's influence had already started. It had begun with an arrow, a Native American symbol of protection, power, and direction. To honor the upcoming birth, my son-in-law, Dan, had bought Cassie a beautiful necklace—a dainty, diamond-encrusted gold arrow attached to a delicate chain.

First was the necklace to honor new life; then, as I pictured the room in my mind's eye, White Buffalo's influence became more apparent as the imagery unfolded from my memory. I realized arrows were everywhere: from the curtain rods to the large wood arrow on the wall above the door opening. The bookshelf held a framed picture with the words "Follow Your Own Path" embedded within a field of six gold arrows of varying sizes. A metal arrow mounted on the wall had "Free Spirit" carved in its center.

Cassie and Dan had painted the walls with large pink, lilac, and purple triangles that blended well with the rest of the arrow motif. The information from White Buffalo suggested a different interpretation of the triangles, and I could see that they looked like the tips of arrows or even a child's drawing of teepees. But every time *I* looked at the walls, I saw an enormous patch quilt.

Even today the walls bring back the memory of the spirit blanket from White Buffalo that covered Cassie. It seemed clear that White Buffalo's influence had begun months before the shared vision with Katherine.

On May 12, 2016, Shalane Grace made her debut. She is a very peaceful, happy child whose eyes are filled with wisdom. When she awakens from sleep, she greets me with a smile that melts my heart. She's small, but powerful. She is fearless and has a voice that is much louder than it should be for her diminutive size. She is usually contented, but if she is not, she will let you—and the neighbors—know. I look forward to watching her grow, knowing that if she chooses a spiritual path in life, she will be guided by White Buffalo.

Dreams, phone calls, lyrics, messages, shared visions, and even room decorations were all reminders of the presence and power of White Buffalo. Each occurrence pushed the boundaries of my belief system a little farther, but nothing compared to the events surrounding Shalane's connection to White Buffalo. White Buffalo did not stop there; he sent a present.

I attended a series of angel meditation classes in July 2015. At the completion of the course, the program's founder intuitively selects a polished stone for each student. These classes are held all over the world, so how could she select stones specifically for people she did not know? I thought she probably randomly selected the stones, but I was wrong.

The stones are typically sent within a couple of weeks after the class ends, but for a variety of reasons, mine arrived ten months later. When I opened the package, I found a white, polished, egg-shaped stone with several veins of gray. I searched the Internet to learn more about it and discovered it was howlite.[19]

A surprise came when I read its alternative names on another website.[20] It seems that my egg-shaped stone is also known by the names sacred buffalo and white buffalo! The egg symbolism escaped my attention until I was writing this chapter. Like a seed,

---

[19] www.minerals.net/mineral/howlite.aspx
[20] meanings.crystalsandjewelry.com/howlite

the egg symbolizes the potential of life and creation; it is a sign of hope for growth.

White Buffalo's impeccable timing did not surprise me. Had the stone arrived, as it should have, at the completion of the angel course, the sacred buffalo/white buffalo names would have been meaningless, because I did not meet White Buffalo until three months later. And there was no egg connection then; it was more than ten months before Shalane's due date.

A gift of hope for growth and new life represented by a stone called white buffalo/sacred buffalo—and it arrived the week of Shalane's birth. I found myself shaking my head in disbelief. I gave thanks to White Buffalo for the present.

I received another message from White Buffalo a month after Shalane's birth. It was on Tuesday, June 14. Summer break had begun a few weeks before, just enough time for my body to accommodate to the welcomed "no alarm clock" mornings; I was finally sleeping past sunrise. I woke up and had my morning coffee as I thought of my son, Phillip. It was his birthday, but due to other travel plans later in the week, I was not able to be with him and his wife, Kelly, in Nashville. As I was thinking about his birthday, White Buffalo's message arrived. It described another birth—the birth of our planet. Because this was Phillip's birthday, I like to think the message was, in part, to honor his birth.

June 14, 2016

We come to speak to you of the elements of Earth. This great Earth is built on a foundation of rock and mineral. At its core is a crystal which is alive; it is the heart of Gaia. Rocks and minerals are our kindred spirits. They have life force just as there is life force in plants, animals, and humans.

The life force of rocks and minerals comes from the energy of power and strength, yet they are guided by the Creator. Gaia was formed; her spirit was birthed by the combination of life-force energy from Creator infused into the crystal at her core, her foundation. The spirit of Gaia sprang forth from this most sacred crystal, laying a path for other energies to come and join the dance of birth and creation.

When the energy from Creator was infused in this most sacred crystal, other energies were called forth. This was the birth of Gaia. She is built upon a foundation of love. The infusion of Creator's life-force energy into her crystal core gave birth to this sacred planet.

Energies were put into motion, and there was a beckoning. From this solid foundation, mountains and volcanoes sprang forth. Waters rained down upon the terra firma. Oceans, lakes, and rivers formed. Animal life sprang forth from the waters in the form of fishes. Grasses, trees, and flowers sprang forth. Great birds of prey were birthed. Four-legged animals began to roam the Earth. There were symbiotic relationships among all of the elements. All lived as one. There was respect for life and recognition of the unity of everything.

Man was introduced to this great planet, and lived as one with nature, for he honored the tenets of life: honor, respect, love, obeying the heart, forgiveness, and harmony. Living by these tenets maintained balance and harmony among all elements of nature. There was mutual respect for each element, for man knew animals, plants, minerals—everything—had a spirit; for the spirit, like man, had been birthed by the Creator and given life-force energy.

This time upon our great Earth, the origins of our beginnings have been forgotten by humanity. A great cloud of forgetfulness covers this beautiful planet. But we say to you, a time of change is near, for the heart of Gaia is awakening.

At her core, the heart of Gaia hears the call of Creator. She is awakening and preparing to blow away the clouds of forgetfulness. Humankind is awakening to the truth within. Gaia is preparing the way for the transformation of humankind. As she awakens, she transcends the era of forgetfulness and brings back to her shores the spirits of the Great Ones that walked the Earth millennia ago. These Great Ones are returning. There will be an awakening for humankind as they realize the truth of oneness of all.

This is a time for celebration. This is a rebirth of the very heart and soul of our Mother Earth. We are honored to be part of this great transformation.

Earth's organic beginnings were sparked when the Creator infused life-force energy into the elements. We lived in harmony, with respect, love, and honor for all. We have traveled far from these beginnings and no longer feel the connection to Mother Earth, much less her inhabitants. The connection to Mother Earth seems to have diminished with each generation, yet White Buffalo speaks of rebirth, a transformation. Humanity is awakening; the *"clouds of forgetfulness"* are drifting, making room for the truth that we are all one. This awakening will return us to a time of harmony with all elements of Earth, including one another.

I felt encouraged by this communication of the rebirth of Mother Earth. I recalled a message from three months ago that reminded me of our divine connection to all there is: *"There is no self; there is only one. The one path. The one spark. To knowingness. To everything."*

In late fall 2016, I had another experience with White Buffalo, but this one added a new dimension to "unbelievable." It challenged and defied my ever-changing definition of reality.

October had ended and I had hoped November would bring cooler weather. The temperatures were still stifling that afternoon as I drove home from work with just enough time to change clothes and pick up Maria. It was the first Monday of the month, which meant attending the crystal bowl Reiki meditation at the Church of Spiritual Light. We arrived at Scott's house and loaded our belongings into his car to make our twice-monthly trek to the church.

We arrived right on time, registered, and settled into areas that we made more comfortable by adding blankets and pillows we had brought from home. We were resting, awaiting the beginning of the meditation when, in my mind's eye, I saw a fine mist cover the room like dense fog. Next, an enormous iridescent spiderweb floated down and sank into the thick fog. As this blanket settled across the room, I felt the energy in the room shift. Everything became softer. There was a sense of silence, stillness, and reverence, and I felt humbled to be witness to this. The blanket also created a loving sense of safety and security, like the love and protection from a mother's arms as she holds her newborn child for the first time.

With the mood of the room established, White Buffalo spoke. He said this blanket of energy represented the Web of Life, and it served as a bridge to connect all there is.

(After I shared this experience with Reverend Bledsoe, she told me of her connection to spiders. Her spiritual name is She Who Weaves the Web, and her online design company is Weaves the Web Marketing & Design. Renee also told me that spider is the "medicine of writers.")

As White Buffalo spoke, I slipped into the vision while I also maintained the role as observer. Within the vision, I looked toward the horizon, and I saw a village of teepees in the distance. At the same time, the observer-me felt a strange sensation in my forehead, like the beginning of a massive headache.

This surprised me because I am not prone to headaches, and I had felt fine when I had arrived at the meditation. I grasped my forehead and willed the sensation to stop, but it did not. My head felt like it had expanded like a balloon, and although the observer-me felt the physical sensations in my body, the "me in the vision" had a different perspective.

Within my mind's eye, my head swelled until it stretched beyond possible limits. My skull shifted and rearranged, morphing into the shape of a buffalo's head. A set of horns protruded from my skull. I watched in total disbelief while the rest of my human body twisted and turned, slipping into the frame of this magnificent animal.

I had become a buffalo—a large white buffalo.

I felt warm, although I stood on a snow-driven plain and sleet pelted my body. I shook my immense head and heard the tinkling of ice crystals embedded in my hair. I could feel the strength and power of my upper body and withers as my cloven hooves pawed the frozen plain in search of a patch of grass to eat. I snorted when I smelled smoke from the distant teepees; the breath left my nostrils in heavy plumes like stacks of steam from a locomotive.

I saw a herd of ponies to the right of the teepees, and one pinto caught my attention. Its white body and large brownish-red spots glistened from the sun reflected off the fallen snow. For some unknown reason, this pony had significance to me. It must have sensed my presence, because it lifted its head and looked into my eyes.

As I glanced at one of the teepees, I saw an inverted spirit teepee stacked on top of it, creating an hourglass shape. I knew these teepees represented the "as above, so below" concept. As White Buffalo, I spoke the following:

November 7, 2016

I exist in this perfect balance between dimensions. The spirit world lies just beyond this blanket of energy that protects it. It is like the frozen waters; the waters are deep, but in stillness, there is reflection of both worlds.

As White Buffalo, I saw myself standing on an ice-covered lake. My reflection mirrored the "as above, so below" concept I had seen with the spirit teepee. Mesmerized, I stood and gazed at my image in the frozen lake as the message continued.

The waters run deep, but in stillness there is reflection of both worlds.
I am power.
I am strength.
I am love.
I am protection.
I am the guardian of secrets of the way of life that once lived in harmony with all there is.
My world still exists; it is just beyond this protective barrier between the dimensions. Open your hearts to the energy, and allow the divine to enter. Enter into this world of power, strength, protection, and harmony. Feel the beat of the drum. Feel the beat of the heart of Gaia. Know that we are all one. Let your heart be your power and strength to guide you. It will guide you with purpose, with balance, with harmony, and with love, which is true power.

There is power in guidance as light from the stars beams down to create a path across the frozen prairie. Look for the signs upon the Earth that have been given to you.

Look and allow guidance from spirit to lead you on this most sacred path of wisdom.

Throughout my journey into these unmarked territories of spirit, I'd had to suspend my beliefs and remain open to hear more. By this time, I had tried to keep an open mind, but none of those experiences had prepared me for this—shapeshifting! Although these events occurred in my mind's eye, they felt as tangible as my everyday reality. White Buffalo opened the meditation by stating he existed in *"perfect balance between dimensions"* and that the spirit world lies *"just beyond this blanket of energy."* This raised many questions for me. Had my crossing of that *"blanket of energy"* into another dimension resulted in shapeshifting? Was it the traversing of this interdimensional energy barrier that had allowed *all* of my spiritual encounters? Had I had become the *"flow-er"* of energy? I thought perhaps so.

As this chapter was coming to a close, the time had come for research. During the months of active communication with White Buffalo, I had resisted any such temptation because I did not want new findings to taint future messages. The Earth and Sky Connection's website has an article entitled "Buffalo Medicine."[21] The prophecy of the White Buffalo has been part of the Native American oral tradition for over 2,000 years, being passed down through generations from the Lakota Sioux Nation. Because it was initially an oral tradition, there are several variations, though the outcomes remain consistent: communication with the Creator through prayer brings needed peace, harmony, and balance for all living things on Mother Earth.

---

[21] earthandskyconnection.com/buffalo-medicine

An article on the Ancient Origins website referred to White Buffalo Calf Woman as a message bearer of the ancestors, but she was also regarded as a healer who brought inspiration, strength, and the power of creation.[22] The Lakota Ranch's website related the legend of the White Buffalo and described White Buffalo Calf Woman as a holy woman clothed in a white buckskin dress. She taught the Lakota Sioux Nation the mysteries of Earth by sharing seven sacred rituals to help guide them on the proper path while on Earth.[23]

The need to search further, for now, had ended. Not only was White Buffalo Calf Woman depicted in a white buckskin dress as I had envisioned her, the messages were similar. The need for peace, harmony, and balance among all living things was reflected in the basic tenets that White Buffalo had shared with me to live by: honor, respect, love, obeying your heart, forgiveness, and harmony. White Buffalo had told me that living by these creeds would help Earth to flourish, to *"help bring back the path of Oneness, the path of Love, the path of Truthfulness"* with the Creator.

Although my explorations into the unknown had led me down many paths, none have been more memorable than my travels with White Buffalo, White Buffalo Calf Woman, and White Buffalo Calf. Their words were unassuming yet filled with timeless wisdom. I will always be grateful for the knowledge they shared with me.

---

[22] www.ancient-origins.net/history-ancient-traditions/white-buffalo-calf-woman-healer-teacher-and-inspirational-spirit-lakota-021067?nopaging=1
[23] lightningmedicinecloud.com/legend.html

CHAPTER 8: THE CRYSTALLINE GRID

As I entered the room, I waited for my eyes to adjust to the dimmed lighting. The echo of my footsteps disturbed the stillness as I approached a body on the slab. The splayed ribcage exposed the internal organs, but this could not be an autopsy or even surgery—I saw myself on the table.

In a state of shock, I looked at my motionless body on the examination table. Something moved; a small pink petal had begun to grow from the center of my heart. It looked like it was from a lotus blossom. A sense of relief washed over me when I saw my chest rise and fall—I was breathing.

The lotus petal grew upward as I inhaled and downward past my supine body as I exhaled. It reversed direction with my next breath and stopped when it entered the back of my heart. The petal's return to its starting point prompted further growth, and the pattern repeated with each respiration. Before long, my chest had filled with more pink petals than I could count, and I realized this looped, circular pattern had formed a torus, a three-dimensional shape with a hole in the center.

As the donut-shaped torus grew, the flower became crystalline. Its pink petals morphed into a milky white substance with glittering gold and white sparkles. I knew it served as a means to prepare my body for healing as it cleared and cleansed my energy field.[24]

This vision occurred at Unity Church of Naples in September 2014. It was my first time to attend this meditation, so I had arrived early. I knew this was a popular event; I had heard my friend Maria talk about Dr. Spano's meditation for years. Dr. Spano is a board-certified physician, and his role for this event was meditation leader. I parked my car in the church's wooded parking lot and headed toward the meeting room. This land felt sacred—even the parking lot.

I entered the hall and took my seat among the few remaining chairs. Apparently I was not the only one who decided to arrive early. I closed my eyes and listened to the soft background music. In less than a minute, however, the time for relaxation ended because the vision with my body lying on an examination table had begun. I grabbed my journal and began furiously writing in an attempt to capture on paper the vivid details as they played out in my mind's eye.

As I was recording the vision, there was an abrupt change in perspective. It felt as if an invisible camera made a 180 degree turn from the activity around my heart to focus on a more important subject. When it stopped, the person facing the me in the vision was none other than Jesus Christ!

He was looking in the direction of the me in the vision while the observer-me watched and listened. He said, "Let not your heart be

---

[24] In the book *Shaman, Healer, Sage* by psychologist and medical anthropologist Dr. Alberto Villoldo described his first experience in seeing a person's luminous body. He described it as a "translucent" and "milky" substance that hovered over the person's chest, with "tendrils" that connected it with others. These features were common to the translucent, milky white, crystalline lotus I had seen growing from my chest—complete with connecting tendrils that reached outward. Villoldo writes that this luminous energy field was "shaped like a doughnut," the same torus field that I had envisioned.

troubled." As if programmed to repeat, the scene of Jesus speaking replayed several times.

I knew these words suggested that all healing begins in the "untroubled" heart. This and the vision of the torus growing out of my heart: I wasn't surprised when the meditation, that had not yet begun, focused on opening the heart to allow healing to occur.

As the recurring clip of Jesus drifted into the background, words began to flow through me, and I received the following:

September 23, 2014

It is the heart center that allows for appropriate flow throughout the energy body. It is the center that cleanses and balances all other centers. Just as the heart pumps blood to circulate throughout every region in the physical body, the heart center is responsible in a similar manner, but instead, using energy. Just as oxygenation occurs in the chambers of the physical heart to renew the blood cells traveling through the body, the heart center oxygenates the energy body by allowing the life force of prana[25] to oxygenate and cleanse the energy body.

The meditation ended and, after giving my thanks to Dr. Spano, I slipped out of the meeting hall. I did not want to socialize. I did not want to talk to anyone. All I wanted to do was to sit in silence to soak in the experience. Jesus? A crystalline lotus flower? These images had surprised me, and I knew I needed time to process what had happened.

As I walked to my car, I found myself automatically taking deep, cleansing breaths. Were these breaths clearing blockages that had been loosened during the healing? As I continued the deep breathing, I remembered the message I had written just before the meditation had begun: the heart center is responsible for oxygenating the energy body. I smiled as I realized that was precisely what was happening.

I had a good night's sleep, and I woke refreshed—not typical for me. I usually get out of bed a few minutes before the alarm rings in

[25] Sanskrit for life-force energy that permeates the universe

order to avoid it shattering the stillness of the room—not because I'm refreshed. Even before I could take my morning wake-up shower, last night's message continued. I grabbed my phone and recorded the following:

September 24, 2014

Blockages must be cleared through the heart to allow fresh, clean, vital energy to flow. Animals live in tune with nature through their hearts. It is through instinct, another word for heart, that animals are guided and know how to behave. The knowing that comes with enlightenment is energy from the heart. Knowing is an energy of clear and close connection between the heart and Source.

These messages supported Jesus's statement that the energy of an untroubled heart was necessary for healing. It was just as the mental vision of the lotus-flower torus had revealed. The spinning field surrounding my heart piqued my curiosity, so I searched "heart energy field" and found the HeartMath Institute's website.[26] This web page describes and illustrates an electromagnetic frequency that arcs out from the heart and then back into it again to form a torus—the exact image I had seen with the lotus blossom surrounding my heart! The US National Library of Medicine from the National Institutes of Health also validated the presence of these electromagnetic fields.[27]

The vision served as a prelude to the next three days' messages. While driving to work early the next morning, the second message arrived:

September 25, 2014

There is a crystalline structure covering Mother Earth; it is a vital, living matrix or web. This one has experienced the crystalline structure in the heart center as it opened and flowed with the energy between her and Source. The crystalline structure is pure energy. When it is connected to spirit, it is crystal clear, and it glistens with

---

[26] heartmath.org/research/science-of-the-heart/energetic-communication/
[27] ncbi.nlm.nih.gov/pubmed/15823696

life-force energy. The life-force energy is alive, vibrant, and magnetic. It draws other energy systems into its field. In its pure state, its structure is crystalline.

Your planet Earth is encased in a network or web connecting it to Source. It acts as a barrier or shield against bombardment of negative or harmful energies. It also operates as a mechanism for humans to connect to each other from long distances via telepathy or other non-senses. Those connections occur between other energy systems in the Earth plane as well as systems outside the Earth plane.

There is a membrane between the various structures of the crystalline grid. Humans have referred to this membrane as the "veil," for it separates the Earth Life System from other dimensions. Those with more direct connections to Source are able to penetrate the veil by projecting a portion of their awareness through these membranes to experience other energy systems (dimensions, realities, etc.). The reaching through the veil is done via nonphysical senses.

Each human is connected to the crystalline grid. This connection is also crystalline; it is often referred to as the silver cord. Those with abilities extending beyond physical senses can view the crystalline connection. Because the crystalline connection is made of living material that is of a nature not seen in the Earth Life System, it is often interpreted as silver in color.

The more humans are able to maintain energy bodies clear and free from blockages, the easier it will be for them to recognize and maintain their connections to the crystalline grid. Humans have many opportunities to maintain clear connections throughout the day by revisiting events, thoughts, and emotions with different perspectives. By reframing these activities and viewing them from higher perspectives, there are opportunities to clear any blocked energy and thus improve connections to Source.

Although I had never heard of a crystalline grid covering Earth, I was eager to learn more. As soon as I stopped my car, I searched "crystalline Earth grid" on my phone and found 4,350,000 hits using Bing's search engine. Not wanting to influence any future messages, I closed my browser.

(Months later, I read several of the websites from that earlier search. Evenstar Creations discusses three main grids operating through and around the Earth. They report both that the crystalline grid consists of portals and doorways that connect Earth to other dimensional worlds, including other planets and stars, and that the crystalline grid is what others have referred to as Ley lines, those invisible geometric alignments that run across ancient landscapes, connecting natural and sacred prehistoric structures.[28] Although the "research" on the crystalline grid did not have scientific backing, I found it interesting that the descriptions online matched the information I had received through the messengers.)

More information was forthcoming; the next morning I received the third message while driving to work:

September 26, 2014

This crystalline grid surrounding Mother Earth is a living structure, alive and vibrant. It is composed of energy, and all energy has life force, making the grid a living entity. Energy systems vibrate at different frequencies, yet each system is alive. The crystalline grid continues to grow in its vibrancy from above and below.

From below, the consciousness of humans, plants, animals, minerals, and all other energy systems of Mother Earth feed the vibrancy of the grid. From above, it is the energy of the stars, solar systems, various comets, and energy from other dimensions including ascended masters and a multitude of other-dimensional beings that help keep the grid vibrant and maintain its protective quality.

Many have great interest in this planet called Earth. It is unique in its characteristics. Many energy systems are free formed without the encumbrances of physical shape, yet within the Earth Life System, we are fascinated to watch energy systems come into existence by entering physical bodies.

With the birthing process, memories vanish. Humans believe they are their physical forms; they are unaware of their true essence (spirit, energy). It is only through working with the human energy bodies (not

---

[28] evenstarcreations.com/index.php/new-earth/earth-grids

the physical bodies) and clearing the energy fields that they begin to glimpse their true nature. It is a beautiful sight, indeed, when we see them blink on with recognition and connection to Source. Humans refer to this event as enlightenment. That is an appropriate term, for we see their frequencies become brighter as they connect to Source.

Many of us are interested in this Earth Life System, and we freely give our energies to help protect it from lower energies that may not support continued growth. We do this by maintaining the crystalline grid. As the grid receives energy, the protections for Mother Earth increase, and connections become more powerful. As humans approach a state of enlightenment, connections become clearer.

Some energy systems have referred to the Earth Life System as an experiment. We do not wish to see it in those terms, for such labeling suggests a sense of disassociation and lack of importance. A human may walk in a deep forest and find an injured animal. The human may nourish the animal back to health, and then return it to its home. This is how we view the Earth Life System. Once energy connections of love and compassion have been made, they cannot be broken. The animal and human may maintain a connection from that point on, although often from a distance. There is a vested interest for the best outcome of the one receiving aid.

We feel a sense of reverence and love for the inhabitants of this energy system called Earth.

The grid is a living structure supported by energies from Earth as well as those with more cosmic origins, and it is designed to protect Earth's inhabitants. I understood that, but I had a difficult time viewing Earth as a cosmic experiment—yet the messengers' description of their vested interest in us somehow counterbalanced my discomfort.

The fourth message arrived while I was driving to work the next morning. I got in my car, buckled my seatbelt, and turned on my phone's recorder. The message came right away, even before I was out of the garage:

September 27, 2014

Many energy systems, including star systems, support the structures within the grid. When this one first connected with the star system from Chiron, it was through the grid, for the grid serves as a communication tool. The crystalline grid is composed of energy— living, vital energy. Unique frequencies in the grid seek specific vibrational matches in order to communicate. Such vibrational matches occurred between this one and the energy system of Chiron, resulting in communication.

The crystalline grid's connection to other energy systems is through streams of energy designed to support different aspects of the grid. The connections also occur at specific junctures within the crystalline grid.

The grid's position is constant, but the Earth's rotation within the grid makes geographic connections problematic. Connections to the grid are made by vibrational matching, and the energy of intent makes communication possible.

Learning that the grid served for both protection and communication surprised me. I wondered whether all the messages arrived through the grid, or only those with cosmic origins. These transmissions left me wondering if I would receive more information on the grid. I would have to wait to find out.

A few weeks later, more information arrived on the grid. This message was tucked among numerous other messages on other topics:

October 17, 2014

The luminous crystalline grid is one of the mechanisms helping with the shift of Gaia. There are new frequencies helping to bring Gaia into alignment with new energy forces stemming from heartfelt energy frequencies, thus helping the ascension process.

New frequencies bringing Earth into alignment sounded familiar. Could it be related to the divergent rays emanating from the sun that I had previously dreamed about?

The luminous, vital crystalline grid draws the energies from the core of Earth—from plant, animal, human, mineral, water, earth, air, fire, all elements. These energies rise and strengthen the interface, resulting in an expansion of Gaia's crystalline core. These are steps instrumental for the shift to occur.

A tipping point will be reached, and the final shift will occur when Gaia's energies combine with those of the crystalline grid. It is the Earth's final step of ascension to the next realm. This new dimension is heartfelt and energy-based. It embraces connection and oneness because it is closer to Source.

When the veils lift, blinders will be removed, and there will be instant wisdom and knowledge. Humans will use their nonphysical senses, leaving brain-based decision making behind. There will be true connection, a sense of realness that they had never felt before.

I felt a discernible shift as a different set of energies arrived, and a vision began. I saw a shaman standing on top of a flat-topped step pyramid in Teotihuacan, Mexico.

(Although I was unfamiliar with Teotihuacan, several months after receiving this message, my son, Phillip, told me this city is frequently mentioned in the television series *Ancient Aliens*. This popular television series reported that Teotihuacan means *"Birthplace of the Gods."* It is known for its flat-topped pyramids, the Pyramid of the Sun and the Pyramid of the Moon.)

For reasons I cannot explain, I knew the pyramid's location. The shaman was brandishing a long rod, the tip adorned with a large quartz crystal. With the staff raised high in the air, he shouted incantations in a language I did not understand. Dark clouds formed in the sky and blocked the sun. Trees bent in the wind, and the sky ripped open as torrential rains swept across the horizon.

The shaman's chants grew louder, as if summoning unknown forces. Bolts of lightning struck his staff, and the crystal glowed as it absorbed these powerful electrical charges. With the sounding of a thunderous boom that reverberated across the land, the energy reversed, and the staff began to shoot electrified energy into the atmosphere.

Like a video, the vision panned back and granted a view from above our blue-green planet. Two other ceremonies were also occurring—one in France and the other somewhere in the Middle East. From my distant vantage point, I saw the lightning from all three pyramids connect at a point far above Earth. The three electrified streams merged and created a large, bright ball of energy. The sphere grew larger until it exploded, and a large holographic pyramid merged from what had been its center.

> *When combined, the series of three connecting pyramids created an interdimensional portal to be used for teleportation to other dimensions. These preliminary steps prepared Gaia to receive the luminous crystalline grid. The shamans installed the foundations for the grid by inserting energy "signatures" for optimal grid placement.*
>
> *This is not unlike what is happening now. Each energy system on Earth (mammal, plant, mineral, etc.) operates as the shamans did on top of the pyramids, connecting to the grid by fibrous energies resembling lightning. The fibers reach toward the grid and, by way of the interface, find their connections.*

The holographic pyramid in my vision served as a teleportation device, a sort of portal used for transportation. Do portals really exist? I had first "seen" them at the Church of Spiritual Light and during other meditations since then, but were they real?

I began an Internet search into pyramids as portals and found sites supporting that theory. Sciforum's website posted discussions theorizing that pyramids were designed to amplify the life-force energy of the buried king to prepare him for teleportation. The air shafts found in the king's chamber in the Great Pyramid of Giza were constructed specifically to allow the king's soul to teleport into the afterlife by way of a star system.[29]

---

[29] sciforums.com/threads/the-great-pyramid-a-stargate.80703

Alan F. Alford tell us that most Egyptologists called these air shafts "soul-shafts" on the assumption that they were used by the king's soul for a direct ascent into the skies. According to Alford's book *When the Gods Came Down*, the soul-shaft theory was initially proposed by Belgian Egyptologist J. Capart in 1924 and the German Egyptologist G. Steindorff in 1929 before being detailed greater by American astronomer Virginia Trimble and Egyptologist-architect Alexander Badawy in 1964. Dr. Zahi Hawass is an Egyptian archaeologist, Egyptologist, and former Minister of State for Antiquities Affairs. In an article entitled "The Secret Doors Inside the Great Pyramid," he reported that Dr. Rainer Stadelmann, a German Egyptologist and former director of the German Archaeological Institute in Cairo, Egypt, believed the shafts were not air vents, but openings "through which the king's soul will rise to the stars that never darken."[30]

Probably the biggest surprise to me was the NASA article "Hidden Portals in Earth's Magnetic Field." Studies completed by plasma physicist and NASA-sponsored researcher Jack Scudder of the University of Iowa report there are magnetic portals that open and close dozens of times each day. Although most were described as "small and short-lived," others were "yawning, vast, and sustained."[31] These portals were places where the Earth's magnetic field connected to the magnetic field of the sun, creating an uninterrupted path leading from our own planet to the sun's atmosphere 93 million miles away. The message continued:

There are multiple ways to connect to the luminous crystalline grid, yet only one path. The path to connection is energy. Humans who can see energy will observe filaments streaming from all living things on Earth. These filaments extend from the animal, human, plant, or mineral, and reach toward the grid. They are guided to connect by the energy frequency signature they carry. They connect to a similar signature, and with use, the connections strengthen.

---

[30] guardians.net/hawass/articles/secret_doors_inside_the_great_pyramid.htm
[31] nasa.gov/mission_pages/sunearth/news/mag-portals.html

There is a way station, an interface, between the Earth and the crystalline grid, a place where the grid and Earth's atmosphere connect. Earth's energy filaments extend into the way station or interface before reaching the grid, where the energy is transformed so it can be directed to the intended location on the grid. At the same time, grid energies extend down through the way station to help with the newly transformed Earth energies.

Within the way station/interface, the transformed energies strengthen and take direction. Their changed vibratory frequencies can connect directly to the grid. This transformation of energy is where the matching of frequencies initially occurs. When there is an energy match, the energies of the crystalline grid, like a hand reaching down to help, gently guide the energy to the appropriate location.

When humans engage in the energy of prayer or intention, the way station operates better. Energy signatures are easier to detect. Without intentions or prayers, the connections are indirect. It is a haphazard approach to match frequencies—much like working a jigsaw puzzle with closed eyes. Intentions and prayers give direction and purpose for the appropriate energies to combine.

This is all for today. With love to this one, we sign off.

The affectionate closing remark brought me back to my initial contact with the messengers. I recalled how uncomfortable I had felt when these connections had started, but because I had avoided making judgments, the conversations had continued. Over time, a mutual fondness had developed.

A month passed without any messages—silence. This was unusual, so I decided it was time to check in and find out why. I got in my car, fastened my seatbelt, turned on my voice recorder, and waited. The following message arrived within a few seconds:

December 8, 2014

It is not that this one is "losing touch" with us as she fears, but she is not tuning in as she did before. The information for this one is always there. There is always a connection; there is a connection via the crystalline grid. The connection is like a telephone call; it can be received with static or without, clear connection or unclear. The energy of communication which emanates from "our side" is of consistent quality. The receiver might have challenges, however. In order to be in a state of receptivity and clear communication, there should be good reception.

A message that has been given to this one for many years is to allow the energy to flow. It is the flowing of energy from the heart center.

At this point, I saw a replay of the vision of the translucent, milky white, iridescent lotus flower that had bubbled up from my heart center—the same image I had seen three months earlier. But this time, a threadlike silver tendril grew from its center; it meandered upward and connected to the crystalline grid.[32]

As you can see, the connection is here; it is always here. It is a matter of setting your antenna to receive the energy of communication.

Now with a secure connection, I tried it out: I asked to speak to my husband and to my father-in-law, who is also in spirit. The message came quickly.

Our hearts are warmed by Lorelai.

Although I knew they watched over us, hearing them speak of my granddaughter Lorelai moved me to tears. This immediate answer encouraged further questioning.

My daughter, Cassie, had been debating whether to leave her current employment. This would be her first significant professional change, and I knew the situation presented a major challenge for her. This difficult decision weighed heavily on her mind.

---

[32] In Alberto Villoldo's book *Shaman, Healer, Sage*, Dr. Villoldo states that shamans communicate with each other through a luminous grid that covers the Earth.

There is nothing that will go wrong, for it is impossible for things to go wrong for this most beloved creature. We are sending waves upon waves upon waves of energy to the Earth plane, providing multiple opportunities to manifest for her.

There is no reason to be afraid. There can only be trust for we are there with her and watching her and guiding her in a very firm but gentle way. We have cleared the path within the field of possibilities. This path will lead in a direction that will be of most benefit to her.

It is a matter of reframing and finding a different perspective from events that have occurred. What might be seen as an unfortunate turn of events is only a jumpstart to put her on a better path. It is not negative, it just "is." It is a matter of trusting our guidance. Know that the dreams she might have and the whispers she might hear are important messages from us.

We send our love to this most beloved child.

Tears rolled down my face, and I sobbed as I recorded the message. As it ended, in my mind's eye, I saw the smiling faces of Cassie's father and grandfather accompanied by my parents and my sister. There were many others in the background—aunts, uncles, and cousins—and each supported Cassie. I took a deep breath and felt thankful for everyone's help.

I had stopped at a red light when the message had ended. As I saved the dictation, I heard an odd sound overhead. I looked through my car's sunroof and discovered a beautiful white egret had landed on top of my car. I smiled and gave thanks for the beautiful confirmation for the message.

During the remaining ten or twelve minutes of my drive to work, both a bald eagle and a red-tailed hawk swooped in front of my car, directly in my field of vision. It was unusual to see either bird while driving to work, and seeing both birds provided additional validation.

I received another grid message about four months later, but this one had more global implications.

April 9, 2015

A path to ascension is to "let not your heart be troubled," for the blocking of vital energy prevents ascension. Ascension is the path of full awareness and awakening into the state of expanded awareness — the ultimate connection to "all there is." By allowing and letting go of negative energies (thoughts, actions, emotions), the heart center becomes disencumbered and is then freed to flow on the beautiful, organic, dynamic path for which it was designed. We have come full circle to the initial message of the "flow-er of energy."

When the heart is allowed to flow, it flows in the direction of Source, and thus blossoms into perfection. Its roots remain grounded while its awareness expands.

Yes, we are coming full circle, for we are all one. It took the ascended master from this one's background to deliver the message. Connection, a vibrational connection, becomes strengthened when the heart is allowed to flow in the direction of Source.

As humans ascend, their connections to Source are boosted by the crystalline grid covering Mother Earth. Many energy systems from outside the grid send specific frequencies to help protect Mother Earth and all her occupants. Think of this as the zeros and ones that are found in computer code.

Embedded within this protective code is a unique set of frequencies specific for humans. As humans begin to ascend, they will learn to select the correct frequencies, like plucking a chosen grape from a cluster. This specific frequency is an energy shortcut, a wormhole into new dimensions.

Your scientists have theorized how wormholes function to connect different realities. This embedded code acts as a lightning rod to catapult humans into other states of expanded awareness. As the human body becomes more crystalline in its composition, the connection to the embedded code becomes easier to access.

Throughout Earth history, humans have been aware of the importance of crystals as conductors of energy; for it is with crystals your first radios were built. Now the connection to crystals is even more pronounced. The crystalline grid and crystalline bodies are more than just crystals, for the crystalline structures are alive, vibrant, and intelligent on their own.

We, the energy system of Chiron and the other energy systems who are the Keepers of the Earth Grid, are waiting with great anticipation as we watch Mother Earth and her inhabitants prepare to enter their next evolutionary step: the crystalline body.

That is all for now.

Keepers of the Earth Grid? A crystalline human body? I needed more information. I found a page entitled "The Earth Grid" on Ancient Code's website that explained how many locations on earth align with the stars. The article suggested that ley lines connect sacred places in an elaborate, planned manner.[33]

In October 2008, English researcher and author Hugh Newman wrote a book entitled *Earth Grids* that describes a geometric energy system that surrounds the Earth. These secret patterns connect many of Earth's most sacred sites. He discusses "great circles" of the Earth that align famous sites like Machu Picchu in Peru, the Giza pyramids in Egypt, Angkor Wat in Cambodia, and the famous moai statues in Easter Island.

The website of Gabriel Cousens, psychiatrist and holistic physician, includes an article entitled "The Human Crystal— Crystalline Properties of the Body," which is excerpted from his book *Spiritual Nutrition*. This medical doctor has embraced the crystalline nature that he says already exists in the human body. Cousens states that by being aware that our bodies are a "series of synchronous, interacting, crystal structures," we can better understand the assimilation of energy in our physical structure. He says the piezoelectric effect of our bone structure acts as an "antenna for all incoming and internal body vibratory energy and information, including direct thought form energy." I was fascinated by this report, especially his ending sentence: "As human

---

[33] ancient-code.com/the-earth-grid

crystalline systems, we resonate in total unity, harmony, and Love with the pulse of the cosmos."[34]

After my Internet research, the messages about Earth Grids and crystalline bodies did not seem so farfetched. Once again, my investigation verified topics that were unknown to me until revealed through cosmic transmissions. With every search engine hit, the boundaries of my belief system stretched farther, and I realized what I had thought I had believed had little to do with the truth. It seemed the paranormal had become my new normal.

I had envisioned this crystalline grid that covered the Earth, and I had learned its multifold purpose. I watched as a crystalline lotus grew from my heart center and connected to the grid around Earth. Changing from a carbon-based body to a crystalline body appeared to be the next evolutionary step.

Regardless of how challenging those concepts were to comprehend, I felt a sense of comfort to know Chiron and other cosmic energy systems were part of the process, watching over our evolution. I smiled at the beautiful ending of their transmission—a message of hope, evolution, and ascension for all of humanity.

---

[34] treeoflifecenterus.com/the-human-crystal-crystalline-properties-of-the-body

CHAPTER 9: ASCENDED MASTERS

While at a healing meditation at Unity of Naples Church in September 2014, I had envisioned Jesus standing in front of me, saying, "Let not your heart be troubled." It turns out that this was the beginning of what would become extraordinary encounters with ascended masters.

At the end of that September, the school year had become arduous, with multiple requests for psychological evaluations, consultations, and staff training. My days were filled with back-to-back meetings. The weekends were equally challenging. In addition to the grocery shopping and household chores, I tried to spend time with my granddaughter, Lorelai, who had turned two in June. Cassie and Dan were very busy, and I knew how much they appreciated some free time that they would not have had otherwise if I were not there to help out now and then. I also tried to speak with my son, Phillip, and his wife, Kelly, on the weekends to try to catch up with their busy lives. Everyone's schedules were full, and mine was no exception. Things seemed hectic as I tried to balance the responsibilities of work, home, and playdates with Lorelai.

Life was so busy, in fact, that I didn't seem to have time for anything else, and almost two months had passed before I realized the messengers appeared to be silent. Had these communications that had burst forth like water through a dam stopped as suddenly as they had begun?

After a two-month delay, one brief message came. Another trickled into my awareness a week later. But on December 11, 2014, the communication door appeared to open wide. I had come home from work and was preparing dinner. As I sliced tomatoes over the kitchen sink for my dinner salad, I felt the hair on the back of my neck rise. I recognized this as a prelude to an incoming message—a shift in energy that alerted me to pay attention. Something was about to happen.

I put the knife and the tomatoes down and automatically took a deep breath. I realized I was smiling in recognition that a messenger was close by—and a messenger who was filled with love and compassion. It was Jesus. In less than one minute, I had received His message, and He was gone.

I walked to my computer, turned it on, and began to type, trying to unravel the message. It was as if I had dropped into the middle of a lecture. After acknowledging that the season was approaching when Christians celebrate His birth, Jesus moved into a discussion about ascended masters, describing them as a group of souls who share higher vibrational energies—frequency patterns that closely align with Source. As souls progress, their vibrations become entrained, matching Source frequencies, and their ascension quickens. Those closest to Source are considered to be ascended masters, such as Himself and the Buddha.

Different vibrational states also exist within the Earth plane. Jesus said that the Earth was filled with lightworkers—those whose energy fields had higher vibrational frequencies than others. These lightworkers were able to influence events by altering energy waves. Healing occurred by adjusting a person's energy to align with the frequencies of health and well-being. Jesus also stated that many lightworkers were aware of the influence that their thoughts had on the environment and on others.

Once I had typed the download from Jesus, I saved it on the computer, then smiled. The messengers were back!

I received information from several different messengers over the next few days, but a week and a half later, Jesus returned with a more direct message. It was the morning after my birthday. I was curled on the couch, sipping a cup of coffee, when I felt the familiar shift in energy that told me a message was forthcoming. I grabbed my coffee, went to the computer, and opened my online journal and documented the following:

December 22, 2014

Lightworkers on the Earth plane are able to sense and manipulate energy in order to effect change. The environment can be changed. People can be healed. Hearts can be mended. The energy fields surrounding lightworkers are different from energy fields surrounding most humans. Lightworkers are aware of the power behind their thoughts. Thoughts create thought forms. Recognition that thought forms are real is the first step in learning to manifest reality.

As lightworkers continue to raise their vibrations, they ascend toward Source. Many different words are used to describe those on this path. I have been called a Messiah. But I say unto you, the only difference is my location on the path of ascension toward the Creator.

People have given many labels to those who are on the sacred path of ascension: masters, prophets, saints, angels, and avatars. As they progress closer to Creator Source, the energy frequency becomes subtler, finer, and lighter. The more closely aligned their energy bodies are with Source, the more enlightened they become. Creator Source, like a great magnet, draws enlightened ones into its field. Many on the Earth plane have reached the prophet or saint status, but they quietly live, going about their daily lives in ways that are not always noticeable.

I made my presence known to this one during a healing session at Unity Church. I spoke to her the words "Let not your heart be troubled," followed by a vision of the life-force energy which is responsible for ascension and purity.

With those words, the message stopped. It made sense to me. When my husband, Daryl, died, I had met two visitors in the Intensive Care Unit's waiting room who had spoken of angels with winged feet. Later that day, the hospital chaplain prayed for the "angels with winged feet" to carry Daryl to his heavenly home. I am convinced that those two visitors were angels disguised as humans.

So, if angels could pose as humans, it was equally conceivable that prophets and saints could live among us. And, for some reason, knowing that the only thing separating us from them was the location on the path of ascension gave me a sense of hope for all humanity.

Once the messages had returned, they seemed to flood my awareness. I learned that if I experienced a silence or lull in the communications, I needed only to quiet my mind in order to receive what seemed to be at the fringes of my awareness. Although the messages had resumed, I did not hear again from Jesus until September 2015. This time, the communications were more personal and accompanied by vivid visions.

It was Sunday, and I decided to take a brisk morning walk. The warm South Florida weather had cooled, and it almost felt chilly—quite unusual for this time of year. I had only taken a few steps on the sidewalk when I began to envision myself among throngs of people standing on rolling hillsides. I knew a messenger had arrived, so I turned on my phone's recorder to capture the images and any words that might come into my awareness.

I could see that all these people were waiting to hear from Jesus. They had gathered in hopes of catching a glimpse or hearing a word from Him. Wearing a long white robe and sandals on his feet, He raised His hand high in the air to quiet the multitude. As His shoulder-length dark hair blew in the arid breeze, He spoke:

September 27, 2015

Seek ye not the kingdom of heaven. Seek ye not the kingdom of Heaven, for in seeking, ye become lost. The kingdom of heaven is not outside of you, it is within. Turn thine eyes within, for the kingdom of heaven is within you; it is you. For if it were not so, I would have told you.

The kingdom of heaven lies within. It lies not in seeking, but in surrendering.

This scene felt real. In my mind, I looked down and saw sandals on my feet. The hem of my long skirt swept the dusty ground as I walked, and hot air blew across my face. Had I traveled back in time? It appeared so.

I felt excitement in the air as His voice projected across the hundreds of people who had assembled. Just His presence radiated grace, wisdom, and strength as He stood before the crowd—the Messiah. Yet I felt His eyes on me as if He spoke only to me, telling me the kingdom of heaven resided within.

The vision ended, and I returned to everyday reality. I continued my walk in silence. This event felt as real as the sidewalk beneath my feet and the palms that swayed in the early-morning breeze.

I got up very early the next morning to walk before going to work. As my feet hit the sidewalk, I envisioned myself back in the rolling hillsides where Jesus had spoken. Had I traveled back to yesterday, or could it have been 2,000 years before? I did not know. As I listened to His words, I stopped walking and turned on my phone's recorder:

September 28, 2015

Dost thou not know me? We have walked upon this Earth for eons. We have walked arm in arm, hand in hand, yet thou dost not know me. Dost thou not know me when thou walkest upon this most sacred and holy ground that our Father hath given us? Dost thou not know me when that gentle breeze bloweth across thy body like the breath of angels, that gentle breeze our Father hath given us? Dost thou not recognize me when thou walkest upon the sands of the desert or the grasses of the fields? Dost thou not recognize me when the songbird sings her melody? Dost thou not recognize me when thou lookest upon the children of this Earth?

I was filled with powerful emotions as He spoke. His energy permeated everything and settled over the masses like a blanket of dense fog. My heart pounded; I realized I had failed to recognize His presence around me. His message continued:

The time is nigh. The time is upon us, for the awakening is here. The time hath come to know who thou art. The time hath come for thee to remember who thou art. Awaken, awaken to the wonderment and the oneness of all.

Seek ye the kingdom of heaven within, for our Father hath planted a divine seed in thy heart, and that seed hath begun to sprout. It hath broken from its shell and reaches for perfection. Transformation occurs as the seed becomes a flower, a flow-er of energy, as its roots descend to this most sacred and holy Earth our Father hath given us. That seedling is reaching to its source. It hath begun a journey of trust and surrender. It thinks not where it shall go; it goes in the direction it is called.

Following the holy path begins in the heart. The germination of the seed from the highest and most sacred Source allows divine guidance to flow. From seedling to flower, as we trust the process and when we surrender our egos, we step on the divine path of awakening.

Later in the afternoon as I walked through my neighborhood, I became aware of an overwhelming scent of red wine. That sensation catapulted me back in time, and in another internal vision I saw myself seated at a large wood table with Jesus and His disciples. The aroma of exotic spices filled the air; we were ready to dine when Jesus spoke:

We break bread together, my Dear Ones, as we have through the sands of time for thousands of years. We gather together in the name of my Father, the most Holy One. We honor our God, for it is He who hath given us life.

We gather together in celebration of the ascension. Yes, the ascension of humankind. We gather together to sup and to plan. We know where we stand. We know we are all one. We know we are united. We know we have awakened, yet there is much to be done. There are many whose seeds of light remain dormant. Why have they not awakened?

They are like sheep, waiting for the shepherd to take the flock into the light of awareness. Good shepherds watch over their flocks with love and compassion. A good shepherd doth not run after a stray lamb but will gently guide it back into the fold. We will be as good shepherds, shining our lights into the masses. We will be guiding stars, calling to those who are lost and who hunger for truth.

My Father hath prepared this table for us, for He is goodness. All who pass by this most holy and sacred table are welcomed, for we are all one. Let us come together and call upon the masses to join us. Let us call upon the masses to awaken and hear the call that stirs them from deep slumber. The time for sleep hath passed. The time for awakening is upon us.

As I returned to my surroundings, I was almost overcome with a sense of awe. I felt as if I had actually been dining with Jesus and His disciples. I had listened to His words of the ascension of humankind, the great awakening. As our divine seeds transform, our lights begin to shine, and we become guiding lights for others who are ready to awaken to their divinity—to the knowledge we are all one, part of the divine spark of the Creator.

I had received a message from Jesus in September 2014, but this interaction with Him was different. Back then, it felt like watching a video clip of Him saying over and over, "Let not your heart be troubled." This time there was actual interaction; it felt realistic yet surreal, far beyond simply observing Him in my mind's eye. I felt as if I were there, participating in these sacred interactions. His words evoked strong emotions deep within me.

Later that evening, I began to read a book a friend had given me the previous week: *The GodSelf: Revelation for the New Millennium*, by Patricia Jepsen Chuse. The book describes the author's dramatic spiritual awakening and her connection to God. The heading on page two captured my attention: "Break Bread with Me." I could not help but marvel at the similarity to the opening statement of the message earlier in the day, *"We break bread together."* As I continued to read, I found other similarities between the book and the messages I had just received from Jesus. These parallels confirmed for me the authenticity of the morning experiences.

History reveals that many avatars and enlightened ones have walked upon this Earth, living as examples and giving us hope. Because of my Christian background, I understood why Jesus was the first ascended master to contact me. But I also heard from other enlightened ones, and a little over two months later, I discovered their location.

It was Saturday morning, and I had just returned from a hurried walk on the beach. The weather was chilly, and I was eager to get home so I could warm myself with a cup of coffee. With a fresh, hot brew in hand, I was sitting at my computer to respond to a few emails when I experienced a spontaneous vision.

I saw myself sitting in a cross-legged lotus position. While floating high above Earth, I moved through a pastel pink and blue gelatinous substance that I knew represented the interface between dimensions. The hectic vibrational frequencies of Earth no longer affected me. I had dropped into a space of stillness—a state of perfect balance and harmony. Although I do not know how I knew this, this place of solitude was called the Realms of Light. With that recognition, I heard the following:

December 5, 2015
I am perfect balance and harmony.

While in this blissful state, I noticed subtle changes as I drifted into an even higher perspective, guided by the vibratory energies of those in the Realms of Light. I looked around and saw ascended masters, guides, shamans of ancient times, star systems, ancient Egyptian gods, angels, and departed loved ones. The silence and stillness of my energy field connected me to these sacred realms, and I knew I could return at will by engaging the vibration of intent/prayer to do so.

I thought of the Buddha, and in an instant, I saw him, acknowledging the stillness and silence that had allowed me to remain in this space of peace. I gave thanks, and within seconds I connected with the disciples who followed Jesus. They told me "the Shepherd" oversaw the changes occurring on Earth.

The Shepherd entered, followed by Mother Mary, Mary Magdalene, and White Buffalo Calf Woman. I saw throngs of angels; power, love, and compassion surrounded them. I was stunned to see extraterrestrials also in this group.

Although this experience stretched the boundaries of reality to the point I thought the seams would burst, I knew the ability to travel to the Realms of Light would be another tool in my awakening-of-consciousness toolbox. I would use this one again.

The messengers told me this experience would be the norm in the not-so-distant future. New incoming energy frequencies were altering the genetic structures of humans and the foundations of Earth, allowing the impossible to become possible. A group known as the Keepers of the Flame served as the forerunners and leaders of this movement, and they were tasked with helping to assimilate these new incoming frequencies.

The messages ended. Still seated lotus style in my mind's eye, I floated back into Earth's atmosphere like a feather in a soft breeze. But before I disconnected from the energy, I gave my heartfelt thanks for this opportunity and especially the knowledge that I could return at will. Although I was back home in three-dimensional reality, something had changed. I felt different; I had retained some of the energy of peace, stillness, and balance from the Realms of Light.

It was a few days before the school district's winter break, and I was looking forward to this two-week vacation. Just a few more days, I thought as I loaded my briefcase into my car for my short commute to work. As I fastened my seatbelt, I knew to turn on my phone's voice recorder. I had felt the presence of a divine feminine energy on the outskirts of my awareness for several days, and today was the day she made herself known to me.

December 15, 2015

I am known by some as Kwan Yin. My purpose on the Earth plane to is to assist in the opening of the heart. I am of divine love and compassion. I represent the mother energy, the birth of enlightenment. I radiate and vibrate the energies of compassion and divine love. I am that energy. I am the energy of a mother who awaits the birth of her child. I am the energy of the mother who nurses her newborn child, giving sustenance for the journey of life. For the true sustenance of life is the energy of divine love.

I had never heard the name Kwan Yin, but a quick Internet search led me to a website called Religion Facts, which told me she is known as the Goddess of Mercy in the Buddhist religion. Some have compared her to Mother Mary in the Christian religion. Both Mother Mary and Kwan Yin personify love, kindness, and compassion, and they are both considered to be miracle workers and saviors in times of calamity.[35]

My presence is strong upon Earth as Gaia is birthing her divine self. Gaia is the mother, and I am but one of her midwives. This is the time for Gaia to enter into her new self, birthed by the feminine energy of all that is. Gaia is birthing new energy frequencies, incorporating them into her life force. It is the age of awakening and rebirth, a rebirth your planet Earth has never seen, a rebirth the universe has never seen.

I have come to this one who has awakened. She is also birthing her new self. I am only a representative of the divine energy that is entering your Earth space. Mary Magdalene, Mother Mary, White Buffalo Calf Woman, and many more of my sisters are part of this movement. As you get closer to Source, you will see our energies are one. We are birthed from Source, as you are. We come together to call forth our divine feminine energies which are needed during the birthing process for Gaia.

---

[35] religionfacts.com/kuan-yin

Another encounter with the divine feminine occurred six months later, while I attended a meditation at the Church of Spiritual Light in Fort Myers. As I entered the meeting room, I noticed altars on the east and west walls, remnants from a previous ceremony. Before I had a chance to sit down, the sight of the altars prompted a vision.

Powerful waves of energy rose from each altar, and they streamed upward and met at the ceiling. The streams of energy blended, fused, and then encircled the room. I felt the energy as it balanced the vibrations in the room and opened the veil between dimensions. Something shifted, and the energy changed to pastel pink as it filled the room with waves of love, devotion, and compassion.

In my mind's eye, Kwan Yin entered the room, and I also detected the presence of White Buffalo Calf Woman. Mother Mary joined them and brought with her an almost overwhelming sense of peace and tranquility. A procession of the divine feminine began, and the room filled with reverence, grace, and quiet solitude. I understood that these energies were making themselves known to those with the ears to hear, the eyes to see, and the hearts to receive. I felt honored to be among those who could perceive these divine energies.

The messenger began to speak, so I found a seat and pulled out my notebook.

May 2, 2016

Rest, Dear One; allow these most sacred divine energies to permeate your body, your heart, your soul.

With those words I envisioned a beautiful pink energy floating down from a point at the center of the ceiling and connecting with each participant. These wave forms from the love of the divine feminine interwove and created a divine pattern of light that drifted in slow motion around the perimeter of the room.

Something called my attention to the center of the ceiling, where the pink wave forms had originated: I saw a splash of red. I gasped when I realized it was blood. I somehow knew it represented the flow of menses from the feminine, as well as blood from the heart.

A spokesperson for the divine feminine came forth and said the energy of the divine Mother lived within this sacred circle, and we needed healing within the heart and by the heart. I realized who had spoken: Mother Mary. She continued:

My love is everlasting. We (all the divine feminine energies from White Buffalo Calf Woman, Mary Magdalene, and Kwan Yin) give to you all the love, healing, and power. You have the power. You are the power. Open your heart and allow this energy to flow to you, to heal you.

It is time upon this Earth that the role of the feminine is honored and called forth to lead. And lead we shall. We shall lead with love. And we shall lead those who are ready to follow. We are all one. Come with us to the divine.

Awaken to the divinity within. Know this is real. With love, we leave this holy space, but know we leave our energy behind. We leave a part of us with you, for you and we are one.

I did not know much about the divine feminine before receiving these messages, but an online search confirmed many sacred feminine principles. In an article entitled "What is the Sacred Feminine?" Amy Peck shared an excerpt from *Voices of the Sacred Feminine,* edited by the Reverend Dr. Karen Tate. The divine feminine represents the dynamic force of creation and of returning to the interconnection and oneness of all. Honoring the sacred feminine reaffirms our connections to the divine, the Goddess, Earth, and one another.[36]

As Mother Mary shared her message, I felt a powerful sense of creativity, protection, and love. Knowing that part of the divine feminine remains with us brought me a sense of gratitude and hope, not just for me but for all humanity.

---

[36] spirituality health.com/articles/2014/12/07/ what-sacred-feminine

After the meditation ended, I asked Revered Bledsoe about the altars in the room. She told me they were part of a Buddhist Wesak ceremony that celebrated the birth, enlightenment, and death of the Buddha. (My later research on the Wesak ceremony revealed it to be a significant spiritual event with powerful effects for humanity. Alice Bailey's book *The Externalisation of the Hierarchy* describes Wesak as a time when two great streams of energy, one from Jesus and the other from Buddha, were fused and blended for the mutual balancing for humanity. The description matched my experience with the "two streams of energy" that "fused" and "blended," validating for me that the experience was genuine.)

I attended a group angel meditation about a month later at the same church. As soon as the meditation began, I saw myself encased in the center of a spinning, three-dimensional shape formed by two pyramids, one pointing up and one facing down. One pyramid spun clockwise, the other counterclockwise. As I floated in this timeless space, the messages began:

June 7, 2016

It is a birthing. This foundation born upon you is a new body, a body of light. It is charged by vibrations of the utmost high. There is nothing it cannot do. There is nothing you cannot do, for you are empowered with divine light.

I bestow upon you the light of the ages, the light that led the wise men to the Christ Child. For this is the light of the divine, the light of wisdom, the light of truth. It is the lighted path of the Buddha, our most beloved Enlightened One. It is the lighted path upon which all ascended masters have trod.

We give to you this roadmap. It is yours. It is within you and always has been. We have only lit the path for you to see. You must take the first step upon this path of wisdom. We are with you, and we shall remain by your side as you traverse this path for which you are destined.

I later learned that this double-pyramid shape was called a merkaba, also known as a star tetrahedron. It was described as a divine vehicle of light that was used by ascended masters to connect with higher realms.[37] It matched the message's description of a new body that is *"empowered with divine light."* Once again, my after-the-fact research confirmed the information I had received. Guidance is within, like an internal GPS that lights the path. But it is only a guidepost, a suggestion. Would I be able to hear the subtle messages, leading me gently down this path of truth and wisdom? Would I be able to step on this divine path and follow it? I hoped so.

---

[37] crystalinks.com/merkaba.html

CHAPTER 10: I DREAMED A DREAM

I came home from college for the weekend in May 1970. When I greeted my mother Saturday morning, she shared her dream from the night before about my sister Jana and a man I will call Mr. Johnson. Jana looked into my mother's eyes and said, "Mama, Mr. Johnson is with me." I did not understand the significance of the dream until the evening newspaper arrived.

As my mother perused the paper, she stopped, looked up, and handed me the periodical that would change my life. I was shocked to see an article that described Mr. Johnson's sudden passing. But this was not news to my mother: she had heard it the night before from my sister who, at the age of twenty-three, had been killed in a car accident a few weeks before.

This became a pivotal point in my life; I could no longer think of dreams as fantasy. Although this occurred decades ago, its impact has remained with me today. This dream brought me two life-altering lessons: When Jana welcomed Mr. Johnson to the other side, I learned we are not alone when we cross into the unknown dimension called death. And when she told my mother of his arrival, I learned there is communication after death.

Mr. Johnson was important to Jana; he was the CEO of the business college she had attended. I felt reassured to know that upon his transition from Earth, one of his recent graduates was there to welcome him to his new life.

Although I had initially categorized my mother's communication with Jana as a dream, throughout the years, a different interpretation emerged. I had learned that this was not simply a dream, it was a visitation. Sleep provides ideal platforms for these visits because we are open and receptive. Our doubts, along with our egos, are tucked away from our awareness, and we allow events to occur without interference from judgment. I have had many visitations, and they have always left me feeling closer to the ones who had passed away. These communications affirmed they were still around and watching over us.

Some of my dreams are precognitive: I experience events before they occur in the waking state. Recently I dreamed I was taking a test with a group of other psychologists from the school district. I had not studied for the test, and I felt anxiety about being unprepared. In the dream, I stated that retirement was near, and I was too old to be back in school taking tests. The dream did not seem to hold much significance, but I recorded it anyway in my dream journal before going to work.

Our winter break had ended, and the school district had scheduled a two-day training session for all psychologists. I arrived early at the school district's administrative center, and within minutes the room was filled with lively conversations as people reconnected and shared their personal stories about their break.

We took our seats as our Coordinator, Dr. Dena Landry, introduced the two nationally known psychologists who would be training us over the next couple of days. With an apology, the instructors began the session by disseminating Scantron sheets that could only mean one thing: a test! And, a test where we would have to pencil in responses in tiny bubbles that are almost too small for my eyes to see.

This was a pretest to gauge our prior knowledge of the subject matter that would be discussed during the training. A posttest would follow the workshop to measure the knowledge we had gained. By design, the pretest covered new information, so it was difficult—very difficult. I whispered to the person seated next to me that I was too close to retirement to feel like I was back in school taking tests. It was only after verbalizing my discomfort that I realized I had already experienced this event—including the dialogue—in last night's dream.

Sometimes in my dreams, I might interact with someone I had not seen in years, and yet within a few days I have an unexpected encounter with him or her. Because I kept a dream journal, it was easy to identify these patterns. When the messengers began to refer to older dreams, I felt a sense of relief that I could rely on the journal instead of my memories.

I received a message in December 2013 about an almost ten-year-old dream. The dream had been so vivid and memorable that the only additional detail the dream journal provided was the date: June 5, 2003. In the dream, I was learning to fly. I have always enjoyed dreams of flying. Sometimes I am the pilot of an aircraft; other times I fly Superwoman-style. When I wake from these dreams, I am euphoric and filled with a secret desire to step outside of my house one day and take flight.

In the 2003 dream, I stood on a large platform that was suspended in deep space. Small groups of one to three people were scattered across the field, and each group had an instructor who was teaching them to fly. I was the sole member of my "group," and my instructor was teaching me to float and glide across a platform that was larger than a football field. No matter how hard I tried, I lost altitude as I crept toward the platform's edge, near the dark abyss of deep space. As I turned around and moved toward the safety of the center of the field, I resumed my altitude of four to five feet off the ground with ease.

When I had the dream in 2003, I had interpreted it as symbolic, about my need to face fears and to learn to trust in myself. But, almost ten years later, I was offered a different interpretation:

December 13, 2013

There is more to this dream than what this one understood. This is a multifaceted lesson. This one has reached the stage where she can perceive more meaning from this dream. Initially, this one knew it was an analogy of life, recognizing that fear can prevent her from achieving her highest desires. We say now there is a different interpretation. The dream can be viewed from another perspective, for she is ready to hear it now.

Humans drop their physical bodies when leaving the Earth plane of existence. The true self is energy. Traveling without the physical body is accomplished with heartfelt intention, but that takes practice. It is thought-generated travel. Thoughts are not produced by the brain, but received by the brain, and it requires laser-like focus to be successful. It takes training. Such training occurred in the [2003] dream, as this one practiced thought-generated travel. Vibrations associated with fear will prevent instant travel. Just as fear lowered this one's body in the dream when she attempted to fly, all lower vibrational emotions such as fear, hate, anger, and jealousy will keep humans from achieving their goals and flying.

When humans enter higher-dimensional spaces, the lighter energies of laughter, humor, love, and gratitude aid thought-generated travel. The dream is preparing this one to travel in other dimensions; her energy body will be ready for flight. All she will need to do is smile and breathe from the heart space, and she will be travel worthy.

The dream she had many years ago represented a lesson meant for two dimensions—the Earth plane as well as the after-Earth plane. It was a dream about learning to manipulate energy to help with flight by increasing the vibratory rate of the energy body.

This newer interpretation fascinated me. In 2003, I hadn't been ready to consider thought-generated travel, but maybe I was now. If the messengers could access old information to give me a different interpretation, did this mean they were responsible for the initial dream? Had they been around all this time, or was this a function of the timeless nature of the interface? It seemed the more I learned, the less I knew. My trip through the unknown left me seeking more information. I recalled Einstein's words, "As the area of light expands, so does the perimeter of darkness."

Who sent this message? As I considered this question, I heard that the message originated from another energy group whose purpose was to illuminate the path of knowledge:

> *Humans state when the student is ready, the teacher will come. We say when the traveler is ready, the path of knowledge will be illuminated. That is why we are called guides, for we guide your journey. As this one's channel widens, more energy groups can communicate.*

An image formed in my mind as the words from the messenger flowed into my awareness, and with incredible clarity, I journeyed back to another dream—this one from the 1990s. Approximately forty people stood in front of me, and although I did not recognize anyone, all seemed familiar. An older man stepped forward and said, "We are part of your soul group."

In the 1990s, I had not heard of soul groups, and I remembered that the comment had puzzled me. The 2013 replay of the dreams from the 1990s and 2003 left me with a feeling of appreciation. I felt confident that members of my soul group had guided me in ways I had never recognized. I wondered if they also played a role that helped me receive messages during the waking state. This message continued:

> *We are from a specific energy group or system that is able to tap into dreaming energies. Each Dreamer has a specific group overseeing him or her, but groups manage multiple Dreamers. Each group contains different vibrations, and each vibration correlates with a specific purpose or task such as dream recall, interpretation, or communication/ translation.*

Less than a week later, more messages arrived about dreaming:

December 19, 2013

This one is surprised she can recall dreams from more than twenty years ago. It is one reason why we encouraged her to keep a dream journal, so lessons could be introduced then and reintroduced years later. She can understand the extended meanings that she was not able to earlier.

It seems the messengers had directed my decision to begin a dream journal. This represented yet another example of the hidden guidance I had received and followed. If the messengers were around and guiding me those many years ago, why did it take me so long to recognize them?

Dreaming serves multiple purposes. One is to release thoughts and memories from daily activities, stored in the form of energy packets or bubbles. When low vibrational energy from stress, discord, and anger are released during the dream state, nightmares can occur.

The inverse is also true. If one's waking hours are filled with higher vibrational frequencies such as harmony, gratitude, and love, the release during the dream state results in pleasant experiences. The more energy released, the greater benefits there are for the human.

Those humans who meditate and engage in positive emotions during waking states are more likely to traverse other dimensions and receive messages of import during the dreaming.

It seemed logical to me that some dreams release stored energy from our daily activities. I have vivid and sometimes negative dreams when I eat spicy foods. Could this be an example of an energy release from daily activity?

I remembered a January 2014 dream. In that dream, I was staying at someone else's house, and I felt a discernible shift in energy each time I exited the bedroom and entered the hall. It was such a remarkable difference that I told others about it and persuaded them to march back and forth with me between the areas. Everyone could feel the difference, and although there were many theories proposed, no one could explain it. As I documented this dream the next morning in my journal, I received the following message:

January 8, 2014

Everything is energy. When humans are dreaming, they operate from a point of reference outside their physical bodies. Becoming aware in the dream state allows the energy bodies, not the physical bodies, to operate. Humans call this lucid dreaming.

It is easy to sense energy shifts from the energy body because awareness is no longer encumbered by the limitations of the physical body. Humans who practice meditation understand that reducing the sensations measured by the physical body can result in the energy body transforming into a spiritual vehicle for dimensional travel.

In the dream last night, this one was able to distinguish energy shifts. We say that she will be able to do this in her waking state once she learns to operate from the energy body instead of the physical body. Operating from the energy body allows a broader view of reality. There was nothing in the dream that separated the rooms that could be measured with the physical senses; it was an energy differential.

Energy is never destroyed, but it can be changed. It leaves its imprint from previous exposures of thought, emotion, memory, and conversation. If a location has been filled with joyful experiences, it will continue to have a positive, favorable impact upon those who enter. The inverse is true for places containing negative energy.

I had never considered the link between dreaming and meditation until I received this message. Both represented states of expanded awareness where the Point of Existence operated within the energy body, not the physical one. Meditation is intentional, but it is more difficult to maintain that same sense of purposeful alertness within dreams. Using the energy body instead of the physical body to experience life would offer a broader perspective, especially when communicating with others. I realized what a powerful tool this could be.

I learned about classifications of dreams a few weeks later. It was Tuesday night, and after an unusually busy day at work, I decided to go to bed early. I fell asleep right away, and I woke the next morning with vivid details of dreams. I got out of bed, showered, and was preparing my pour-over coffee when a message began. I went to my computer and documented the following:

January 28, 2014

There are different levels or classifications of dreams. This one is learning to connect with what is referred to as the instructional dream state. Some dreams are precognitive, foreseeing future events. Some precognitive dreams are specific; others are symbolic. All humans have precognitive dreams, but not all can recall them. This one had a dream about rabbits, which seemed to hold no significance for her at the time.

The previous week, I'd had a dream that took place in a beautiful meadow filled with wildflowers. I was lying on a spacious blanket, watching large white clouds move against a blue sky. With no warning, thousands of rabbits hopped on and over my body as they crossed the field; I was in the center of a bunny migration. The weight of their little furry feet as they jumped on my body reduced me to giggles, but any significance to the dream beyond its entertainment value escaped me.

A few days later, this one received toy rabbits. The purpose of this dream was to demonstrate the precognitive nature of dreams: rabbits in the dream followed by rabbits in the Earth plane.

A couple of days after the dream, a neighbor had given me three gifts for my granddaughter, Lorelai: a porcelain statue and two stuffed toys—all rabbits, testifying to the precognitive nature of the dream. This realization brought to mind the numerous precognitive dreams I had experienced over the years. I remember dreaming that Roxanne, an occupational therapist I worked with, was pregnant. I saw Roxanne the next morning and shared my dream. Her mouth dropped open in surprise as she sat down on the couch in my office and confirmed what I had learned in my dream. She knew I had not heard this from anyone else, because she and her husband had not yet made the news public.

Events are offered to humans via the dream state prior to manifestation in the Earth plane. This is mostly recognized with the onset of major events such as the Great Tsunami of 2004 or the 9/11 attacks in the United States. Because Earth plane events of great magnitude affect large numbers of humans, many had foreshadowing via their dreams. Most insignificant precognitive dreams, such as with the gift of rabbits, do not rise to the level of wakeful recall.

The interface between the dimensions is where Dream Seeds/Dreamers collect and recognize these not-yet-manifested energies. As humans awaken, the interface is more accessible, and dream recall improves. The Dreamer/Dream Seed is a subset of lightworkers who are instrumental in guiding masses through the final shift into the next dimension. They are charged with helping others recognize, acknowledge, understand, and interact with their dreams on more conscious levels.

The message ended. I saved my entry in my online journal and turned my attention to the coffee I had been preparing. I couldn't help but wonder about the messages. Dream Seeds? Dreamers? What did that mean? My questions were answered later that day.

I returned from work and changed clothes to take a short beach walk. I often listen to music on my phone while walking. This seemed to be a perfect setup: if a messenger arrived, I switched to my phone's recorder and used the built-in microphone on my earbuds to record the communication. As I passed other people while walking, it would appear as if I was engaged in a phone conversation. If they only knew!

I had walked only a few hundred feet when I recognized a messenger was close, so I opened the recorder. My questions from earlier in the day were about to be answered:

There is a subset of lightworkers called Dreamers or Dream Seeds. A planted seed expands. Roots extend down, anchoring the plant in the ground. A seedling emerges from the seedpod, extending upward and breaking through the soil. The soil is similar to the interface into the next realm—from earth to air. Similar to this process, seeds must be planted in one realm (dreams) for manifestation to occur in another realm (Earth plane).

When a plant breaks through soil, it has reached a new dimension, yet its roots remain anchored in the seed's source dimension. Dream Seeds are similar, for they operate within the interface connecting two dimensions while still rooted in the Earth plane.

As this one continues to develop her role of Dream Seed, the interface between full consciousness and the dream state (also referred to by humans as the veil) becomes more accessible.

What did *"continues to develop her role of Dream Seed"* mean? I hoped more information would be forthcoming—and it was. There seemed to be a break in communication, so I thought the message had ended. I continued my walk and switched back to my phone's music app. About ten minutes later, the message continued:

The work we do with humans during dreams affects them during waking states, but most are unaware. This one is awakening and is able to bring dream energy into wakefulness. We commend her for this work.

The description brought me back to the first communication about the flower. We are flow-ers of energy, and when we are in perfect alignment with below and above, we blossom into fullness. A few hours later, the message concluded with one brief sentence:

And now the Dream Seed and the flow-er of information have come full circle.

Three days later I had an instructional dream where I was taught how to choose an appropriate outcome from a field of probabilities. By using the power of my intention, I could connect with the probable outcomes in any given situation and choose the most favorable result. I woke up from the dream and began to record it in my online journal before getting ready for work. However, the following message, which included elements of the dream I had been attempting to record, interrupted my thoughts. I saved what I had completed in the dream journal and opened the messages document to record it:

January 31, 2014

This one has seen various energy clusters in what humans refer to as empty space. Everything around humans is energy. Nothing is empty. "Empty" space can be compared to a gelatinous substance; every movement in it has a rippling effect. This includes not only actions in physical bodies but energy movements via thoughts and intentions.

The dream demonstrated how training occurs in the dream interface. The interface connection of the dream state is the most familiar format for Dreamers/Dream Seeds. Dimensions are bordered by barriers. When the barrier of one dimension (dream state) connects with the barrier of another dimension (wakefulness), an overlapping field of energy is created. It is within this interface that the Dream Seeds maintain awareness.

Some humans can maintain awareness between dimensions during meditation and prayer. Psychic mediums operate in an interdimensional interface. Others, such as this one, have become channels. The channeling of information also takes place in the interface. There are some humans who enter trance states during channeling. This occurs because their connections in the interface are more substantial. They travel so far into the other dimension that it overshadows the current dimensional awareness.

Interface connections are growing stronger as Mother Earth transitions to the next dimension. As Mother Earth passes through the interface, she brings all humanity and other living beings with her.

This one has participated in instructional dreams. She has now graduated from the Sleepers class and is now part of the Dream Seed class, where she is more lucid in the dream state, and the connections become more obvious. She will find her dream journal is of value. Many seemingly insignificant dreams gain significance when viewed through the eyes of a Dream Seed. Some dreams become important with recognition of their precognitive nature. There are lessons learned of how energy shifts and rearranges in the interface prior to manifesting in the physical plane, much like the Phoenix who rises anew from ashes. Setting intentions in a dream will result in observable manifestations through energy exchanges. The interface between dreaming and waking life grows.

We send information to this one in her dreams as well as her waking states. She is transitioning to a subtler realm of energy in which to function. Those nonphysical connections (dreams, channeling, and meditation) are easier to access because of her elevated vibratory status. She is learning to use her intent during the dream state. This has happened many times in the past but without her awareness. She has graduated from the basic Sleepers class, because her awareness has increased. She is now waking during the dream interface, and now is a Dream Seed.

Graduated? It seemed all those lectures I remembered attending in my dreams over the years had been beneficial, and my dream journal had proved to be a valuable resource.

A February 2014 dream served as another Dream Seed lesson: A bird was trapped in my house; it beat its wings against the sliding glass doors and windows of my living room in a frenzied attempt to escape. When it tried to fly out an open window, the window's screen blocked the exit. While the bird fluttered against the window screen, I closed the window to prevent the bird's retreat back into the house. My actions trapped the bird in the space between the closed window and the screen, so I had to reach my hand *through* the glass of the closed window in order to open the screen to set it free.

That same night, I dreamed I had entered some sort of museum that had a large gallery displaying hundreds of crystal clusters of varying sizes, shapes, and colors. The vibrant colors seemed more intense than any I had seen in "real" life. I received messages about both dreams the next morning.

February 8, 2014

Dream Seeds can maintain the connection between dreaming and wakefulness. The dreams last night were part of the review process common in instructional dreams. This one is engaged in review exercises as part of the instructional dream state. There were two scenarios in last night's dream: one involved the freeing of a trapped bird, the other the awareness of crystal clusters.

This one reached through the window pane to free a bird. It is not possible to penetrate solid matter on the Earth plane, but it is a common occurrence in our dimension. The bird was trapped between two spaces; it was in the interface. The interface connects two dimensions, and this connection allowed for energies to open doors to the next dimension.

Physics on Earth apparently differ from the physics in other dimensions, making the impossible possible. Will we abide by these laws of physics when we transition from Earth when we die? Were these instructions preparing me for something specific?

In the dream involving clusters of crystals, this one acknowledged colors unlike those on the Earth plane. The energy of crystals in our dimension has always been welcomed and acknowledged. Crystals are instrumental in the Earth plane as well, due to their healing powers as well as their ability to raise vibrations of objects within their energy field, including humans and animals. This is why a large crystal exists in the core of Mother Earth.

A crystal at the core of Earth? I decided to investigate. On the Pittsburgh Supercomputer Center website is an article entitled "Understanding the Earth: Crystal at the Center of the Earth." Geophysicists Lars Peter Stixrude from the Georgia Institute of Technology and Ronald E. Cohen from Carnegie Institution of Washington hypothesize that Earth's center is crystalline. The outer core of Earth, about two-thirds to the center, is molten iron. But at Earth's center, the pressure is so great (3.5 million times greater than the Earth's surface pressure) that the iron solidifies. In a study that took over two years to complete, Stixrude and Cohen researched the different varieties of iron's standard forms. By supercomputing seismic data, they determined that "the temperature-pressure extremes of the inner core offer ideal conditions for crystal growth." From that research came the theory that the center of Earth was composed of a single giant crystal. These results were published in *Science*, one of the world's top academic journals from the American Association for the Advancement of Science.[38]

The message continued:

Many objects in our dimension appear different from what humans perceive in the Earth plane. This is because the original is in our dimension. The Earth plane holds only a shadow of the original. Humans who have been in our dimension through near-death experiences, deep meditation, visions, or dreams confirm these findings. In our dimension, colors, sounds, and tastes are enhanced because humans are no longer limited by their physical senses. This is what happened with this one in her dream last night. When she perceived the crystal clusters, noting the colors were beyond anything she had witnessed before, she had traveled beyond the interface and had entered our dimension.

In the other dream, she was represented by the trapped bird in the interface as well as the one who released it. This was symbolic of her freeing herself from the confines of the interface and accessing our dimension, and it was accomplished through her volition and abilities as a Dream Seed.

She has been in our dimension many times, but as a recent enrollee in the Dream Seed class, her awareness has increased. These are the beginning steps. Previously taught lessons are reviewed, but this time with awareness. She is now aware of the reason for journaling her dreams. What were thought of as inconsequential dreams over the past

---

[38] psc.edu/science/Cohen_Stix/cohen_stix.html

years were exercises, often symbolic, in either the interface or in our dimension. The difference now is her awareness and the immediate translation of symbolic imagery.

Dreaming is an ideal platform for learning. With the logical mind asleep, information can flow freely, and the lessons are not hindered by judgment. Dreams may include scenarios that might be considered bizarre in waking reality, yet they appear quite natural in the dream state.

The Dream Seed messages continued. The "review class" ended about a week and a half later and made room for new information to arrive. I heard a series of beeps as I woke one morning. My first thought was that one of my electronic gadgets required my attention—and then I received a message that the sound would be explained. I opened my phone that was next to my bedside and recorded the following:

February 10, 2014

The tones introduce new incoming energy patterns. The Dream Seed class has moved beyond the requisite review, and new material is introduced. This was an introduction. The beeps or tones are a form of communication using interdimensional echolocation, not unlike the echolocation of whales and dolphins. The tones prepare this one's energy body for advanced travel within our dimension. Deep interdimensional space is filled with energy that is much subtler and finer than what is found in the dream state.

In order for this one to navigate farther into our realm, she requires vibrational adjustments; these are performed by the tones. Just as tuning forks or drums produce sound waves that can be felt with the physical senses, our tones move through the energy body to align the subtle energies in a pattern conducive with the vibrations deeper within our dimension. Her energy body will be more receptive to our frequencies, and she will be able to recognize and understand newer vibratory patterns.

The new communication codes are finalized; but she is not yet able to translate or understand those messages. We are in the beginning stages of the process. As she spends more time in the dream state with us in the intermediate class, her vibratory nature will adjust and accommodate to the new frequencies introduced. And as her energy body adjusts to the newest vibratory patterns, input from other messengers will be understood. As part of the Dream Seed class, all lightworkers are prepared to understand other-dimensional communications.

When I was younger, dreams had held no significance for me until my mother's dream that I shared at the beginning of this chapter. That is when I realized these successions of images during sleep could represent an entry into another world. The messengers told me about Dream Seed classes and the Sleepers class.

Only recently had I remembered the classes held during sleep time. I wondered if lessons also occurred during waking states, but perhaps below the level of conscious awareness. As if my thoughts had invited an example, I received another Dream Seed lesson almost a month later, and this time the lesson occurred while I was wide awake. It was another lesson on echolocation.

March 6, 2014

The energy associated with thoughts is instrumental in this lesson. Fine-tuning has occurred through the introduction of new patterns as established by interdimensional echolocation.

Once connections and adjustments have been made with other dimensions and energy systems of finer vibrational substances, travel occurs by setting an intention of the destination. You are immediately there, unless you prefer a slower method such as floating. These are examples of intentions and the power of the energy frequencies of those intentions.

Due to the density of the Earth plane, many do not consider intentions as energy, and they go about their lives with little regard to the power of these heart-based thoughts. Not only are intentions instrumental for travel in our plane, they are used to connect and disconnect from other energy systems. If there is an energy that you wish to disconnect from, the connection can be blocked by using imagery.

Any imagery will work. Humans can imagine their bodies as large molecules with specific receptors. Assigning an energy system to a specific receptor allows the opening and closing of the connection by thought. Covering or plugging receptors prevents connections. There are innumerable images that can be used to achieve this goal.

If all spirit connections need to be blocked, the human can shield the entire energy body. It is very much the same for individual energies requiring blocking but on a more specific level. Imagine the spirit's energy field as a beam of light approaching your energy field. Any means to block the path of that specific beam will be effective. Thoughts are energy. Energies will combine and follow the actions put forth by your thoughts. It is such a simple and easy process, yet the dense energies of the Earth plane prohibit most humans from recognizing and acknowledging the power of energy associated with thoughts or intentions.

It has been established that this one is a student of the Dream Seed class. Today a lesson is shared with her during waking hours instead of the dream state. We are assigning homework consisting of listing five different visual scenarios in which one can block unwanted spirit connections.

Yes, I completed the assignment, and as I did, an uncomfortable memory of graduate school flashed before my eyes. And like school, a couple of days later the assignment was reviewed.

March 8, 2014

Our assignment demonstrated how energy works in our plane. All inhabitants in our plane are composed of finer frequency patterns as thoughts and visualizations are in the Earth plane. While on the Earth plane, thoughts have an associated energy with them, and they are real in that sense. But do not confuse the origin of thoughts with the common fallacy that they are generated by the brain. Thoughts are received by the brain, based on the energy connections. In our dimension, because the inhabitants are also made of the same vibrational frequency as the thoughts and visualization, these thoughts are reality.

In our dimension, thoughts become things, and learning is immediate. Just as an Earth child learns the word "hot" if someone speaks the word when the child touches an open flame, the lessons in our plane are immediate because of the direct connection between action and response.

As this one continues Dream Seed lessons, she will spend more time in our plane, and when she returns, she will be able to effect changes with thoughts. When she makes her permanent transition to our plane, she will be adept in our ways.

There are children born in the Earth plane with strong connections to other dimensions. They are not blinded by what humans refer to as the veil. More are coming to the Earth plane with clear connections to other dimensions, and they are using the power of their thoughts to change physical matter. Some children are healing Mother Earth's children (people, plants, animals, minerals, waters, and atmosphere) as soon as they enter the Earth's dimension. Others levitate physical items. All of this is part of Mother Earth's transition.

The information about newer generations coming to Earth with stronger psychic abilities didn't surprise me. There are even names for these children: Indigo, Star, Crystal, and Rainbow children. Each generation seems to be more psychic; perhaps this is because there are more awakened parents who encourage their children's special abilities. Many enlightened parents understand that their children may hear and see things that are beyond what physical senses can measure, and that these new abilities allow their children to interact with invisible playmates or angelic spirits. A beautiful learning opportunity occurs when parents listen to their children and encourage further conversations.

In my generation, many children who mentioned they saw their deceased grandparents, invisible playmates, or angelic beings were often told they were mistaken. This closed the doors of communication from both the parents to the child and the child to the other-dimensional beings. In my work as a psychologist, I have spoken with many young parents who seem willing to accept their children's expanded skills. Perhaps times are changing.

I stopped recording the message and begrudgingly pulled out the vacuum to begin weekend housecleaning. I was more than a little relieved when the message began again; it offered a break from my chores. What I had thought was an abrupt end to the previous message had simply been a pause.

In our dimension, healing occurs on a molecular level. Our healers know the origin of a specific ailment or dis-ease, and they make changes to the molecular structure. This is common in our dimension. Those who have awakened to their connections with other dimensions can learn to do this.

This one is learning these things because of the lessons from the Dream Seed class. The more she spends aware time in Dream Seed classes, the more her energy mirrors ours. All Dream Seed students can heal humans by perceiving the root cause of the dis-ease. Because Dreamers can perceive a wider range of subtle energy frequencies, they approach the root of the problem with extreme precision and specificity. They can make changes at molecular levels, quark levels, and in DNA strands. We offer an analogy.

And with that, another visualization began. I saw a shining pile of sun-colored sand on a large piece of glass. The golden grains reflected and refracted light like diamonds; it reminded me of a miniature mountain from a children's fairy-tale book.

Then the sand scattered across the smooth surface, as if blown by a giant's breath. It leveled the gilded mountain to a single layer of individual grains. The shifting sand brought a new perspective, as red, black, brown, and green grains of sand that had previously been hidden came into view. I understood the analogy offered in my vision: discerning divergent sand particles represented finding disturbances at the cellular level in the human body in order to heal the root of the disease.

Our energy is finer; our perceptions are not blocked by solids. We see energy subtleties which make it easy to make adjustments and corrections to the root of the energy disruption which created the disease.

The blending of these states of awareness is due to this one's increased sensitivity to our energies. This has both positive and negative effects. This one will be more sensitive to Earth plane matters that can result in overreaction to emotionally based energies. Yet the positive effect is the ability to bridge other dimensions.

This one's connection to our dimension is altering her basic energy patterns. The result is that she is becoming a beacon to others in the Earth plane. Other humans are seeking connections with her. The beacon quality of her energy is a result of the Dream Seed, the seed that represents the connection between the dimensions. As the seed grows and blooms, it draws others like a blossom's invitation to insects. The bloom of the Dream Seed is a beacon for seekers.

As this one pulls other energies into her field, protective adjustments are needed. We have shown her how to block connections to unwanted energies. She needs to learn new protections from Earth plane energies. She knows this on an intuitive level, but she needs time to process and to learn to achieve a higher level of protection.

Lessons received in the next few nights in the dream state will be specific to this topic. And, yes, she does continue to spend time in both dimensions during her waking state. We will be there as guidance to help her in this adjustment. Humans are guided and drawn to her for a reason, and she must make alterations in her human goals in order to balance her new role as Dream Seed.

About a week after I had learned to search for the root of a problem by discerning disruptions at the cellular level, I had an opportunity to practice. On March 14, 2014, while gathering my belongings to drive to my friend Marilyn's house, I had a spontaneous vision. I saw a three-dimensional picture of nerves running from the center of Marilyn's neck, down her back, and into the trapezius muscle. I looked at it with interest. Why had the messengers showed me this? The nerves looked like the intricate root system of a plant. My eyes were drawn to several dark clusters located at the tips of several nerve endings. I immediately understood these represented the roots of pain and discomfort, and I knew what to do.

I saw myself getting smaller. I felt like the incredible shrinking woman from a science fiction movie, and I continued to contract until I was small enough to stand in front of the darkened nerve endings. I looked down at my miniature body, and I noticed I was sporting some sort of laser gun that reminded me of the supersized water guns my children had played with when they were younger. Instinctively, I raised the laser gun and zapped a dark nerve ending, reducing it to smoldering ashes. With a flip of a switch on my handy-dandy, supersized laser gun, I followed with an icy-cold blast to neutralize the area. I moved to each nerve ending and removed the cause of the pain at the root of the problem.

When I arrived at Marilyn's house, I was not surprised when she told me her neck had been bothering her. I knew exactly what to do. Just as I had practiced minutes before, I visualized energy going to the nerve endings and I neutralized the pain. It worked; Marilyn's pain stopped.

My long-standing interest in dreams continued, but the messengers gave me a greater appreciation. Dreams were much more than topics for interesting conversation. Over the past few years, I had begun to see dreams as platforms for a variety of experiences: precognition, instruction, communication, interdimensional travel, and expanding consciousness. The next message offered another function of dreams, and it seemed to be a continuation from a message that surfaced in response to a dream in January 2014. Although I knew that many dreams offered a review of daily events, this new message expanded that notion:

September 3, 2014

Sometimes a dream contains elements that occurred during the waking state of that day. This is because the energy packets from the events of the day (actions, interactions, thoughts, and emotions) seek a niche within the energy field, preparing it for recapitulation. This occurs during the waking state and the sleep state, although most humans are not aware.

Humans who are Dream Seeds or Spirit Weavers maximize the dream recapitulation process. It is a part of this rearranging of the energy packets that is often observed in the dream state. For others, the energy packets are placed in a queue to be accessed during the waking state, but only awakened ones can effectively engage these processes.

While the physical body sleeps, the energy body is active, arranging the events of the day into coherent patterns, including the energy of interactions and thoughts. The energy remains in place until the human reaches a state of heightened awareness, when the physical body is ready to drop away as the human transitions to another dimension.

Dreams occur in the timelessness of the interface where the rules of physics and time do not apply. When this one recalls dreams from years ago, the details remain because of the timelessness of the interface when the dreams occurred.

Introduction of the term *"Spirit Weavers"* surprised me, and although I expected clarification, none came. Over time, however, I had learned to trust the messengers, so I knew they would share more information when the time was right.

I continued to document dreams in my journal, knowing that the seemingly unimportant ones might present different meanings in the future. For example, a dream on April 24, 2015, held no specific value for me, other than containing something from a previous dream: a clock. It was a typical battery-operated clock, the type that I might have traveled with twenty years ago as a backup to a hotel's wakeup-call. Many clocks look alike—but without knowing why, I recognized it as the same clock I had seen in a previous dream.

As I typed the entry into my dream journal, a download came about the thinning of the interface between the Earth and other spiritual realms. As the veil thins, overall awareness increases during sleep as well as waking life. I'd had recurring dreams before, but these were only ones that held some sort of significance. Recognizing the reappearance of something as insignificant as a battery-operated clock suggested to me that my awareness and lucidity had increased during my sleep. With that realization, the following brief message arrived:

As this one continues her spiritual path, there will be further examples of this thinning of the veil. It is good that she recognizes these events for what they are.

With the thinning of the veil, it seemed that I had gained more access to the interface through meditation and the visions that often accompanied the messages. More time in the interface resulted in better dream recall, and that enabled me to remember downloads during sleep. Before then, the only downloads I could recall were those that occurred during waking hours. Spending more time in the interface brought a memory of my friend Alan, a gifted psychic medium. Although he had passed away in 2008, that didn't prevent him from dropping in for a visit.

Alan appeared in my mind as I drove home from work one day in 2014. His appearance evoked a memory: He had often stated that he spent more time on the other side than he did in Earth's reality. As I recalled this memory, Alan said that my situation was similar, and I couldn't disagree. The intensity of the Dream Seed classes resulted in me spending more time in the interface than in the three-dimensional reality of Earth.

I had an inkling of the impact the thinning veil had on my life, and I wondered if others would be affected as much as I had been. Would this mean that humanity would be exposed to endless possibilities as other-dimensional energy entered through dreams?

My fascination with these nocturnal visions began with my mother's dream in May 1970, with a specific communication from my sister Jana who had recently died. My mother's dream taught me that we are not alone when we cross the great divide between Earth and the next dimension. This offered great solace to me, and it altered my view of life. There *is* life after death, and communication *is* possible. My interest in dreams continues but with broader implications.

Dreams are the interface between reality on Earth and the possibilities contained in the next dimension. The dream state offers a judgment-free platform in which to receive insightful information not often available during waking hours. Many inventions, discoveries, theories, and creative works of art have originated from dreams, including the discovery of the periodic table, the scientific method, the theory of evolution by natural selection, proof that nerves transmit signals chemically, and multiple mathematical theories.[39] Famous books, music, films, and scientific discoveries, including the discovery of DNA, the Beatles' album *Yesterday*, and Robert Louis Stevenson's *Dr. Jekyll and Mr. Hyde* were products of their dreams, according to the website Mental Floss.[40]

The valuable lessons I have learned through my dreams have enriched my life. I am thankful for my awareness of at least some of these activities and the possibilities that present themselves through dreams that may not be otherwise available.

So, perhaps it is time for us to dream, and in doing so, we can explore other worlds of endless opportunities and bring these other-dimensional ideas and energies into our lives. Our dreams can open doors to these magical realms filled with boundless ideas that can bring positive change for all humanity. Perhaps it is time to open the doors to see what dreams may come.

---

[39] famousscientists.org/7-great-examples-of-scientific-discoveries-made-in-dreams
[40] mentalfloss.com/article/12763/11-creative-breakthroughs-people-had-their-sleep

CHAPTER 11: IN THE BEGINNING

How could I explain the unexplainable? How could I share this story with others when I had trouble believing it myself? My experiences confused me, yet they filled me with awe.

My life transformed in the early hours of September 29, 2015. The hundreds of messages from star systems, angels, and ascended masters that had stretched the boundaries of my reality paled in comparison to this. I struggled for days to process and understand the meaning of this event. Each day I received another bit of the puzzle, but on the fifth day I had an epiphany, and the pieces fell into place and formed the completed mosaic.

An enormous influx of energy had invaded my body earlier in September, and for weeks I had become a whirlwind of activity. This took me by surprise. For weeks, my customary eight to nine hours of sleep were reduced to two or three each night. As a psychologist, I am aware of the effects of sleep deprivation, especially when lack of sleep becomes chronic. Memory may be affected as fatigue sets in and thinking can be impaired. But this did not happen to me. I went to work and functioned well—in fact, better than usual. I felt alert as I moved through my days with a sense of clarity that surprised me.

Later, I researched this paradoxical effect. I discovered in the National Institutes of Health's database (PubMed), a study

(PubMed ID: 9779520) where REM sleep deprivation can lead to enhanced mood as well as increased energy and alertness. Researchers studied twenty-six healthy, normal volunteers with no history of sleep disturbances. For five nights, the volunteers stayed in the laboratory, and after gathering screening baseline data, they were subjected to "deprivation nights" to prevent REM sleep. Evaluation of the volunteers revealed that prevention of REM sleep did not cause a loss of alertness or increase of sleepiness during the waking state. Perhaps that is what happened to me: my decreased sleep disrupted the REM sleep phase.

What was this extraordinary energy that had invaded my sleep? Could this be a prelude to something related to the messages? Would it introduce a new messenger?

After another brief sleep in mid-September, I got out of bed around 2:30 a.m. Driven by the same energy that had interrupted my sleep, I put on shoes and shorts and went outside. I felt compelled to run.

Although I had been a runner in high school, that ended with my first back injury in 1986. Months after the injury, I still required help to get out of bed, and I could not walk unassisted. After multiple spinal surgeries, my back and neck contained enough hardware to set off security machines at airports, so my decision to run shocked me. Why did I think I could do this?

But run I did. I jogged almost a mile on that first day, and by mid-week, I had increased my distance to three miles. This felt incredible, unbelievable. What made me do this? Why and how was I doing this? The sudden and unexplained surge of energy seemed to be preparing me for something big.

Then it happened: While I was running at 3:00 a.m. on September 29, 2015, a detailed event played in my mind's eye with such clarity that I felt I was actually in the scene. I stopped dead in my tracks. Although I was motionless, I felt a sense of swift movement, as if I had fallen into an abyss. Darkness surrounded me, yet within the vast, black void, almost imperceptible movements seized my attention. Black shadows as dark as the void itself drifted like transparent chiffon scarves caught in a slow-moving night breeze. Only the motion of the dark clouds enabled me to distinguish them from the void.

The pattern became more defined as the momentum of the swirling clouds increased and coalesced into a whirling haze. As if on some silent, invisible cue, the energy rushed from all directions toward a central point where a small glimmer of light began to glow.

Seemingly in response to this ember of light, the incoming clouds became frenetic and formed roiling waves that raced toward one another. I expected them to collapse together, but instead, the waves reversed direction and arced backward. This motion created the three-dimensional donut-shaped circle of a torus field. The actions seemed to energize the light, and it became brighter than a thousand suns.

The frenzied movement came to a complete halt, as if someone had paused a movie. Yet I was still there, and I existed in the absolute stillness of this suspended world. Then I saw an ever-so-slight movement in the light, followed by another and another, until the light began to throb like a giant heart. A new life had been born.

I experienced another moment of total stillness, as if life herself had held her breath. This tranquil instant ended with an incredible explosion: the beating heart burst into billions of light fragments that spread across the horizon as far as I could see.

I wept. I knew I had just witnessed Creation.

This incredible vision continued and expanded. Over the next several days, the original scene replayed in my mind. I would get up early and walk or run before work to try to offload some of this extraordinary energy. And each morning, I received messages that offered different overlays or interpretations of the initial vision. I learned of matters that had been foreign to me: black holes, singularities, gravity wells, wave forms, cosmic voids, dark energy, expansion of the universe, sacred geometry, stargates, event horizons, entrainment, photon belts, and how stars were formed.[41] I saw Creation as it related to Christianity, energy, science, physics, quantum mechanics, and astronomy.

I had no explanation for these bizarre events. These experiences differed from anything that had happened before. I was besieged with questions: Why, and the more important question was why me? What should I do with this information? I needed answers.

Answers came after the fifth day of instruction. Early Sunday morning on October 4, 2015, the messenger explained the reason for the multiple overlays I had received: I had become an "instrument of the word." When I heard this phrase, the prayer of St. Francis of Assisi came to mind, "Lord, make me an instrument of your peace."

In my role as an "instrument of the word," I realized I had been named an agent, a representative. I was to be a translator for the new energy—the same energy that had been responsible for the vision of Creation. Different interpretations meant reaching wider audiences through a shared vocabulary. This also raised questions about the other messages. Did my role as translator apply to them as well?

By chance, a few hours later I learned that this day, October 4, was the celebration for the Feast of St. Francis of Assisi. I could only shake my head in disbelief at this fortuitous discovery; this revelation offered credence to the message. As I smiled at this unexpected finding, these words came out of my mouth with no warning: "I see the Light."

The Word

In the beginning, God looked about and saw nothingness, for there was nothing and is nothing except Him. There was no form. There was no space. There were no boundaries.[42] He is. He is all that is. There is nothing more. As He is everything and everywhere, there is nothing,

---

[41] archive.ncsa.illinois.edu/Cyberia/NumRel/BlackHoleAnat.html
[42] Cosmic void

no thing where He is not.[43] Yet there was a desire for expression, the expression of His Oneness.

Therefore, He called forth the formless energies of all that is to come to Him. He did this with a great exhalation of breath.[44] His breath continued to the far reaches, awakening His life force, and throughout everywhere, the energy obeyed the summons. And so it began.

He then inhaled, using His breath to pull those energies toward Him. This inhalation created a vacuum.[45] With the reversal of His breath, the energy contracted; it became a magnet for those formless energies, pulling them to His center.

Those energies swirled in all directions, gathered together, turned, and raced toward the Source of the call. And from all directions, those energies came.

Megalithic waves came forth like a gigantic tsunami, gathering strength and force as they raced toward the Source of the calling. As the waves approached the center of the vortex created by His summons, they crashed into each other.[46] Waves of dark energy collapsed into particles.[47] The energy began to enfold upon itself, creating layers upon layers,[48] flooding into that deep center of stillness, the vacuum that had called them home.

The outer waves of energy continued to contract and rush toward His center. The great toroidal field of energy relentlessly circled then collapsed, repeating the pattern of building and collapsing, over and over. This great vortex, this boundless vacuum, gathered more and more photons of all that is until it formed the first black hole.[49]

The crashing of these energies into the center of the Creator produced awareness. Rising awareness observed as form grew from the formless; boundaries developed, creating space where no space had

---

[43] Representation of the Holy Spirit
[44] Expansion of the universe caused by dark energy
[45] Gravity
[46] Gravity well
[47] Quantum mechanics, wave forms collapsing into particles
[48] Donut-shaped torus field
[49] Gravity produces black holes.

existed before there were boundaries. Awareness created consciousness.[50]

As the torus continued to build and recycle energy, its center became more powerful as awareness and consciousness intermingled and increased astronomically. Yet stillness, centeredness, and holiness filled with power and love resided deep within the center. This ever-building field of dynamic energy created energy fusion, a nuclear reaction of these mighty energies.[51]

This nuclear reaction, this massive shift of energy, produced light, brilliant and powerful beyond measure.[52] These great energies created a single point of light and energy called the singularity.[53] A star was born.[54]

This singularity, this brilliant star, exemplified the awareness of God—the Creator, expressing. It represented the life force of our God, consciousness, creating the great central sun/star. This great light began to beat like a giant heart, taking on a life of its own. Its vibrations matched the music of all that is.

At this point, I had a vision of hundreds of thousands of diamonds scattered on a black fabric that stretched for miles. I noticed movement from underneath, as if an invisible hand had pinched and tugged the material downward. In response to this gravitational pull, the diamonds rushed toward the center and spilled over the rim of the opening. They tumbled into the mouth of the black hole like water down a drain before they disappeared into the center of the vortex. Within moments, the clustered diamonds had created a brilliant single point of light, the singularity.[55]

---

[50] Our Father, born of the Holy Spirit

[51] Nuclear fusion creates energy in the core of stars. Without gravity to contain the energy, a star explodes.

[52] Nuclear reactions produce high-energy photons, the elementary particles of light.

[53] A singularity is located deep in a gravity well at the center of a black hole. It is theorized that the Big Bang began with a singularity.

[54] Waves in molecular clouds cause nearby gasses to compress and form stars.

[55] A black hole is created by strong gravitational fields, produced when matter has been compressed into a very small space. The force is so strong that nothing can escape: an event horizon. Singularities are said to exist in the centers of black holes.

His energy continued, creating more awareness and consciousness, strengthening the singularity, that great central sun/star, even more. He looked at what He had done, and this pleased Him. He smiled and said, "This is good."

This was the birth of the universe. It was done, the ultimate manifestation of energies: Creation. Light was born out of the energy of consciousness and awareness of all that is.

The star of the great central sun/Son was formed.[56]

But it did not stop there, for our Father gathered this single point of existence, the light of the singularity, His sun/Son from deep within the center of His stillness. He commanded, "Let there be light!" With that, He hurled the light across this new universe with His breath of life, prana, the energy of life force.

An explosion of the light of the singularity followed, an explosion of His awareness, an explosion of consciousness, extending beyond immeasurable boundaries. The singularity shattered and created an event horizon.[57] As the center of this star exploded, it created a stargate.[58]

From the center of our Creator, energy exploded into spaces not previously known, for there had been no space before our Father commanded light to come within. And now, He had sent his sun/Son, His light, across the ocean of nothingness into the infinite beyond, past the confines of the newly-birthed universe, spreading both particles and waves of energy. Yet ever so faint, the heart of the singularity continued to beat.

In an instant, the light of the singularity washed over all that is. Many humans refer to this as the Big Bang.[59]

---

[56] The Son was born.

[57] An event horizon is associated with a black hole. It is a boundary in space-time where gravity's pull is so great, nothing can escape.

[58] Theoretically, a stargate is a type of wormhole created by the excessive gravity of a black hole.

[59] The holy trinity was completed. Father had birthed consciousness/awareness from the Holy Spirit, and now the Son/sun was born. From a scientific perspective, the theory of general relativity proposes that the Big Bang began with a singularity.

Energy from above crossed the soul of the singularity, extending below to anchor both dimensions through the energy of conscious awareness, creating the "as above, so below" concept. The horizontal explosion of the singularity produced an energy beam of consciousness that anchored the "as within, so without" dimensions. At the center of both the vertical and horizontal pillars, the soul of the singularity continued to beat, sending life-force energy to all that is. The trinity was completed, and the totality of its components shattered with the explosion of the singularity, spreading the holographic particles of all that is to all there is, but its essence remained and continued to pulse.

Never before or since has there been such a massive eruption. The Creator hurled His own sun/Son from the center of His being into the new universe. As the energy from His sun/Son exploded within the newly formed universe, the multiverse formed.

Those exploding divine sparks from this great star created another dimension. The energy of the "as above, so below" and the "as within, so without" became conceptualized as a great, multidimensional star, a merkaba, the great symbol of life from which all life sprang. It came to symbolize the energy and power behind all of Creation.[60]

And so it began. We were created from light. Those pieces of the divine light are the star seeds that were sown, for light that was scattered from the beginning came from the great central sun/Son, a great, magnificent star. We are those sparks of light, shot forth from that sacred stargate. We are pieces of the singularity.

But as the multiverse expanded, the trinity began to separate until the point where we became lost. We strayed from the flock of the One Most Holy. We knew not from whence we came. We lost our homes, our sense of belonging, our true nature. We no longer knew our divinity within. We knew not that we came from light. Like sheep that had wandered from the fold, we found ourselves lost in a wilderness, alone and afraid.

---

[60] The merkaba is a star tetrahedron, created by combining two pyramids, one pointing up, and the other pointing down. The merkaba is part of sacred geometry; it is the pattern for all Creation.

The two pyramids of the star tetrahedron separated; one moved up as the other moved down. This created space and the perception of separation. This gap between the two pyramids became known to humanity as the veil. Humanity no longer felt connected to the Creator, our separation caused by the veil of forgetfulness.

The separation of the holy trinity continued as the multiverse expanded, caused by the shattering of the great central sun/Son. The end result: many humans live their lives unaware of their connection to Source, to home, to light, to the Creator.

But many are awakening to the truth that we are those flames cast off from the All-Mighty expression of energy. We are created from the magnificent light source, the great star, the great sun/Son of the universe. It is a part of us, and we are a part of it, for we have come full circle.

There was a new light, a new set of energies that were cast off from the great central sun/Son during Creation. Yet this energy was different. It remained intact as a huge photon belt. This photon belt is now part of the ascension process for it is awakening the star seeds within each of us. The energy of the photon belt is similar to the energy of Source.[61]

I wondered whether the energy of the photon belt was what I had felt. Was this what had filled me with this incredible energy and granted me the vision of Creation?

The Shepherd is calling us home, back into the flock from which we came. As this new energy reaches us, entrainment occurs.[62] *The star seeds deep within our hearts are starting to vibrate to these new frequencies, taking on more light, awakening from the deep slumber which has held us captive in a sea of forgetfulness. As our frequencies entrain to the newer energies, the ascension process awakens. Our*

---

[61] The photon belt is interdimensional light that passes through the Milky Way Galaxy every 26,000 years. Some believe Earth will pass through this belt of light as part of a spiritual ascension.

[62] Entrainment is the process by which interacting systems become synchronous.

universe is no longer expanding but beginning to contract as we chart a course home to Source.

We are not separate from all that is. We are all one, for we have been birthed from the light, and now it is time to return. It is time to know our Source, to recognize our Source, to love our Source, and to return to Source. It is time to awaken to our divinity within.

Look upon this sacred symbol and know ye are God. This is symbolic of Creation, of return to the great central star/sun/Son within. It is symbolic of the New Order of Melchizedek which has come upon the Earth at this time to awaken the ascension process within. Ye are born of the great central sun/Son. Allow that sacred star seed within to awaken.

Come, dance with me. Dance with me in this light that shines ever so brightly from within. Come dance with me through this beautiful new energy that has been given to us. Come dance with me, oh, ye children of the light. Come dance with me in the light.

In the beginning, the messages about the flower and my experience with the royal poinciana tree had evoked feelings of apprehension, and it had made me feel afraid and helpless. I didn't know what to do; I had no plan, yet in doing nothing, something happened. Within that quietude of nothingness, the energy flowed, and the open door invited more messengers. Before long, I recognized the wisdom within the messages as well as the value of the inadvertently opened door of spirit. As I acquiesced to the role of messenger, I realized I had become a flow-er of information.

I could have never imagined that these strange beginnings would have led me to another even more significant beginning: Creation.

Why me? Why had I been given opportunities to see beyond everyday reality into that mystical space outside of what the physical senses measure? The answer had arrived: I was an instrument, a representative of the word of the messengers. As an agent for the messengers, I had been assigned the task to interpret and unveil these words to those who were ready to hear. Yet these lessons and ideas would be shared through *my* words.

My words. These were not the words of a prophet, an ascended master, or a saint, but the words of a common, everyday person who had stepped onto a path into the unknown. I may never know the reasons why I had been chosen to be a representative, but I realized my acceptance of this challenge had transformed me. As I processed these new responsibilities, the boundaries of my life as a reluctant messenger dissolved to make room for this new role—this role that had changed my life's course from an ordinary path to an extraordinary journey that had already enriched my life beyond measure.

AFTERWORD

When Candice Sanderson came into our space for the first time, I don't think either one of us knew that our destinies were about to meet. I shall never forget the experience. We have a very unique space. It is an interfaith, all faith- no faith sandbox temple for the soul. We used to call it a place for mystics without monasteries, but then we became that monastery. Intuitive, soulful, and telepathic connections are nothing new to the people who find their way to our space. But something was definitely different about Candice, and I knew it right away.

As she and her friends (who have now become our dear friends) came for our crystal bowl meditation, I recall that it was a crowded night. There wasn't much floor space left, so I was sitting in the chair at my desk which is on the peripheral of the room. Candice ended up taking her spot not too far from where I was sitting. From the moment I laid eyes on her, and that is saying something because the room was very dimly lit, I was struck by this simple but very clear guidance: "Pay attention to her." And so I did.

From that moment on, I felt as though I was en pointe, and Candice was the focus of my attention. But it was not like one might imagine. I simply turned my chair to face the room, and even though she was about five feet away from me, I felt very near to her. It was a very gentle connection, almost like a coalescence. It had this protective quality, as well. As you can see, sometimes words fail the mystic! I had not consciously done this before with someone during this meditation. It was highly unusual, since the biggest part of what I do concerns holding space for the whole group. To be guided to single someone out in this way was not the norm. But it felt, for lack of a better word, destined; yet at the time I had no idea what it was all about.

During the meditation, I myself did not have a visualization and neither did I go "out." It was a strange mixture of deep peace and silent, subtle communion without any sense of the actual communiqué. I did not really feel linked or tethered to Candice. I simply felt present, available and attentive to her. In fact I received no cognitive psychic response from her. It even felt like she was oblivious to me in the physical, as if I were invisible to her. So when the meditation was over and people began to share their experiences, even though I knew that I had been somehow connected to Candice, I was in awe when she began to speak about what she had experienced during the meditation.

As Candice began to share, I realized that she was "picking up on" all the symbology and imagery that we have been working with for years. These are things that we not only study but work to embody. I realized that at the heart of what she was describing, she experienced and "saw" images and artwork that is located in a special meditation room where we were hosting a John of God Crystal Healing Bed. She was so precise in describing the artwork, which happened to be the Masters that we work with, that I asked her if she was sure she had never been here before. She said no, and I knew that she had not, but it is always good to stay grounded in these matters.

As she finished telling me what she had seen, I then informed her that she was describing our John of God Crystal Healing Meditation room. To which she or one of her friends responded that Candice also has a John of God Crystal Healing Bed in her home! Needless to say, we felt the pull of this convergence as the synchronicities anchored and grounded us into this most powerful experience in the present moment. I asked her if she wanted to come see the room. I don't think anything would have stopped us at this point!

As we went into the room, I pointed out the paintings on the wall, both of which she had described. The most prominent one was White Buffalo Calf Woman; the other one was entitled "Ode to the Medicine Wheel," which was what she had described. She had tapped into so many subtle and not-so-subtle things. For example, she described a giant white spider that spun a beautiful, protective web. I was quite sure that she did not know that my spiritual name is She Who Weaves the Web, and that my web design company is named Weaves the Web Marketing & Design. I told her this and also that spider is the medicine of writers. Our community works with writing very much behind the scenes in the inner journey work that we do. This was something she would have had no way of knowing. And since she had not written a book at the time, she was not yet an author. Looking back I see that spider was giving her a great gift. For as I mentioned prior, the mystic can be deeply challenged to bring their experiences into the world of words.

Needless to say, Candice would come back and visit our space, each time revealing new and even more profound spiritual connections between what we had been transmitting and transforming for years and what she was visioning. But the pieces were obviously still being put together. There was a longer period of time when we did not see Candice. It was during this time that the person who owned the John of God Crystal Healing Bed that we were hosting moved it out of our space. In the ordinary world, this would have represented a disaster since we featured the bed at our holistic healing fair and also offered private sessions in our beautiful Himalayan Salt Meditation room.

When we first began hosting the bed, there were only two in our area. But since that time, I did see that some people had been acquiring them. So I began to look into other options. A few inquiries later, without finding a good fit, I just surrendered it. I knew that our part was to provide and hold space and that it was not our part to purchase a bed—at least not yet. And I knew the reason why, for our entire philosophy is centered around true community and spiritual partnerships. I knew it was important that we keep ourselves in a position of co-creation with the community and the people. Nevertheless, when the stakes are high, letting go can be a challenge. So after having no luck with finding a replacement bed, I was left with just letting go and trusting that the Universe would provide.

Hip deep in this process of trusting, I suddenly remembered Candice and that she had a crystal healing bed. I understood that she had it in her home and was using it more for her own personal healing, so perhaps that is why it didn't come to me straight away to contact her. Then there was also the problem of how to contact her. I did not have her full name, nor phone number. She lived an hour away from us in the next city and I did not, at the time, know how to contact the other people she had come with. Then I remembered that the first time she came to our space, at that time about a year prior, I had asked her to email me the write-up of her experience that first night. I knew she had written it down as she was taking copious notes immediately after the meditation. So I could hardly wait to sift through my email history, praying that I would find Candice's email. I was thrilled when I found her message and gathered up the courage to ask her if she would be interested in bringing her John of God Crystal Healing Bed to our monthly fair.

It didn't take long for Candice to respond, and I was so grateful and surprised when she said that she would be very interested in doing that! I was not sure at all that she would say yes to this. Our relationship had really mostly been etheric. There was not an ounce of physical, verbal or written contact (except that one email), even though it appeared that we were close enough to be telepathically linked. I joke now with her that I wasn't sure she even liked me! I think that I was definitely picking up on her reluctance as a messenger. It was almost like she didn't know how to take what was happening to her. Even though it was miraculous and wonderful, it can also be overwhelming and even confusing to experience the world of spirit on a more grounded and real basis, as she was doing. So you can imagine my absolute shock and awe when she went on to tell me that she had written a book and that I was in it!

Our mystery school and monastery provide the sacred space for spiritual work and esoteric teachings. But Candice didn't have any idea that we are something of an outpost for those who are ready for higher teachings. This is not publicized. One of the things that must have come online for our students to be ready for such transmissions is a measure of intuitive awareness. A new earth mystery school cannot be found through ordinary means. That very psychism and willingness to follow the subtle instruction of the soul is what pulls the seeker there. Hence the great admonition: Let those that have the eyes to see and the ears to hear, see and hear the truth.

We understand, through a history of attracting people into our space who have shared visionary experiences, that the noosphere is alive and well. We are creating and co-creating with each other. In our monastery we focus on experiencing the Ageless Wisdom Teachings of the Great Masters. It is our philosophy that these beings who have become masters of matter are of great value to us who are in the evolutionary states of becoming fully human. In the Munay Ki tradition this is known as Homo Luminous or light body. All the great mystery schools and traditions have their name for such. The way that these masters communicate with us is quite subtle at times, coming through a feeling or knowing. But there are many other times where the communication whether through meditation, symbology, imagery, direct insight, tracking synchronicities or shared visioning and journey work, is profound, clear, concise, and unmistakable.

The people who have gotten to know Candice in our community, as she has begun to share her story, see her as an affirmation of our interconnectivity. Because of her beautiful ability to be the scribe of her experiences, she has provided an indelible link between our two worlds. In the years our community has been forming, we have often spoken about and recognized those who would come as being connected long before they came in the physical to our space. Candice, because she documented, dated, and wrote her experiences, has shown us that this is absolutely so. With so very many intricacies and interweaving of our stories, it has all become very grounding. And out of the grounding comes a great sense of comfort and stability in "walking the worlds." Because the great truth of the laws of manifestation, and most notably here the law of attraction: That which is like unto itself is drawn. This is how we find our way home, not just manifest a new car.

Candice's appearance in our community, to us, is nothing less than a part of our collective soul retrieval. She has brought a crucial aspect of this group home to us through her very own authentic and individuated Self. Often it has been stated throughout the years that we are a community of writers. Candice has truly opened this door in a way that can speak to the hearts of those for whom this message is intended. She is living proof that our spiritual work, and all spiritual work, can find its footing in the world, if we are paying attention and if we will allow it.

It is with overwhelming gratitude and joy that I write this Afterword for Candice's book, *The Reluctant Messenger*. Even that is divinely given, because Candice and I stood apart from each other holding witness as sacred bookends on a line of communication that happened outside of the cognitive thinking mind and the concrete physical world. Most people struggle with their inner life, chalking their dreams and visions up to wild imaginings. But we are so lucky because we get to ground them in our reality in a way that is healthy and good, creating positive and powerful things in life with the energy and information it brings to us through true community. Each person holds an important place. The place that Candice holds in my heart, and I might dare say in the heart of us all, is to trust our subtle senses, open to the "more" of life, be filled with wonder, and above all—write it down! Reluctant or not, Candice's message to us is one straight through the heart that joins us together in a way that is real, relevant, creative, healing, and profound.

Rev. Renee Bledsoe
Minister and founder, Church of Spiritual
Light and Blue Star Monastery

Founder of Addiction Alchemy: Universal Medicine Wheel

Rev. Bledsoe's upcoming books 2019:

Humanity: The New Messiah

Addiction Alchemy: Universal Medicine Wheel (A Next-Generation Recovery Model for the New Earth through Tribal Community)

Your Vibe Attracts Your Tribe (101 Ways to Raise Your Vibration on the Universal Medicine Wheel)

ACKNOWLEDGEMENTS

I would like to express my gratitude to those who helped make *The Reluctant Messenger* possible. Several sets of eyes helped me write, polish, rewrite, produce, and publish. A big thank you to my sisters Marcia Williams and Eleanore Zurbruegg and to my friend Roberta Moore for being the grammatical gatekeepers and finders of errant punctuation. I am especially thankful for my editor, Jennifer Razee, whose wise comments and suggestions helped refine my words into a relatable story.

I will always be grateful to Maryna Zhukova at MaryDes for a book cover that magically captured the essence of the manuscript. A special thanks goes to Dr. Doug Heatherly at Lighthouse24.com for coming to the rescue when interior formatting issues arose.

I am grateful to Dr. Laurin Bellg for the Foreword and her unceasing encouragement. I thank Reverend Renee Bledsoe for the Afterword and for developing my website (CandiceSanderson.com). I am proud to consider both of you my friends.

Last but not least, I send my appreciation to Clark Press and The Muses Within. Without their guidance, this book might have remained a series of correspondences recorded on my phone. I could not have done it without you. Thank you!